A Plain Protestant's Manual, Or, Certain Plain Sermons on the Scriptures, the Church, and the Sacraments, &C

by John Wood Warter

A PLAIN

PROTESTANT'S MANUAL,

OR, CERTAIN

Plain Sermons

ON

THE SCRIPTURES, THE CHURCH, AND THE

SACRAMENTS, &c. &c. &c.

IN WHICH THE

Corruptions of the Romish Church

ARE EVIDENTLY SET FORTH.

By JOHN WOOD WARTER, B.D.

CHRIST CHURCH, OXFORD,

VICAR OF WEST TARRING, SUSSEX,

Rural Dean, and Surrogate.

" All this I have done simply and plainly, without all show of learning, that it might the better sink into your hearts."—BP. JEWEL.

" We have much better employment for our hearers than these controversies, did not their restless endeavours to pervert men make it sometimes necessary."—ABP. SECKER.

" Trouble yourselves with no controversies willingly, but how you may best please God by a strict and severe conversation."
JER. TAYLOR.

London:

FRANCIS & JOHN RIVINGTON,

ST. PAUL'S CHURCH YARD, AND WATERLOO PLACE.

1851.

"All these novelties which she hath invented and intruded into the Church, she colours them with the show of ancient custom, and so, very craftily, under the name of antiquity, fights against antiquity."—Bp. Cowper of *Galloway.*

"Let us therefore a little discuss the several differences, and (as it uses to be done, when the house is too little for the stuff) let us pile all up close together. It shall be enough, in this large harvest of matter, to gather a few ears out of every shock, and to make a compendious dispatch of so long a task."—Bp. Hall, "*No Peace with Rome.*"

"Let the vain sophistry of carnal minds deceive itself with idle subtleties, and seek to elude the plain truth of God with shifts of wit : we bless God for so clear a light, and dare cast our souls upon this sure evidence of God ; attended with the perpetual attestation of His ancient Church."—Ibid. "*The Old Religion.*"

"I am not to judge of men's persons : many are called Papists, who know not what Papist means ; and may live Papists, who dare not die Papists ; or, if so they do, they know not what they do."—Bp. Cowper of *Galloway.*

TO THE

PARISHIONERS

OF

WEST TARRING, HEENE, AND DURRINGTON,

SUSSEX,

𝕿𝖍𝖊 𝕻𝖑𝖆𝖎𝖓 𝕻𝖗𝖔𝖙𝖊𝖘𝖙𝖆𝖓𝖙'𝖘 𝕸𝖆𝖓𝖚𝖆𝖑 𝖋𝖔𝖑𝖑𝖔𝖜𝖎𝖓𝖌 𝖎𝖘

WITH EVERY FEELING OF SINCERE ATTACHMENT,

(AFTER A TRIAL OF SEVENTEEN YEARS,)

GRATEFULLY INSCRIBED,

BY

THEIR AFFECTIONATE PASTOR AND FRIEND,

JOHN WOOD WARTER.

ΠΕΡΙ ΤΟΥ ΜΗ ΔΕΙΝ ΑΝΑΘΕΜΑΤΙΖΕΙΝ.

Εἰ τοίνυν ταῦτα γεγένηται παρ' αὐτοῦ, καὶ τούτων τοὺς τύπους ἡ ἐκκλησία πληροῖ, καθ' ἑκάστην ὑπὲρ πάντων τὰς ἱκετηρίας ποιουμένη, πῶς σὺ τολμᾷς τοιαῦτα φθέγγεσθαι; εἰπὲ γάρ μοι, τί ἐστι τοῦτο ὃ λέγεις 'ΑΝΑΘΕΜΑ; ὅρα ὃ λέγεις, ἐπίστασαι τί φῂς, ἔγνως τούτου δύναμιν;—Ὁ Ἀπόστολος ἐν δυσὶ μόνοις τόποις τὴν φωνὴν ταύτην ἐξ ἀνάγκης φαίνεται εἰπών, οὐχ ὁριστικῷ δὲ προσώπῳ ταύτην ἐπήγαγεν.—Ἆρα τὸ τυχὸν εἶναι τὸ τοιοῦτον ἡγεῖσθε, τὸ πρὸ καιροῦ καὶ κριτοῦ τῇ τοιαύτῃ ἀποφάσει καταδικάσαι τινά; τὸ γὰρ 'ΑΝΑΘΕΜΑ παντελῶς τοῦ Χριστοῦ ἀποκόπτει· ἀλλὰ τί λέγουσιν οἱ πάντα δεινοὶ τὴν κακίαν; ΑΙ'ΡΕΤΙΚΟΣ, φησὶν, ἐκεῖνος γεγένηται.—Δι' ὃ δέομαι ὑμῶν, μὴ παρέργως τῶν τοιούτων λόγων ἀκούσητε· τὰ γὰρ αἱρετικὰ δόγματα, τὰ παρ' ὧν παρελάβομεν, ἀναθεματίζειν χρὴ, καὶ τὰ ἀσεβῆ δόγματα ἐλέγχειν, πᾶσαν δὲ φειδῶ 'ΑΝΘΡΩΠΩΝ ποιεῖσθαι καὶ εὔχεσθαι ὑπὲρ τῆς αὐτῶν σωτηρίας· γένοιτο δὲ πάντας ἡμᾶς τῆς περὶ τὸν Θεὸν καὶ πλησίον ἀγάπης ἀντεχομένους, καὶ τῶν δεσποτικῶν ἐντολῶν τὴν ἐργασίαν πληροῦντας, μετὰ ἐλέους καὶ φαιδρῶν λαμπάδων ἀπαντῆσαι ἐν ἡμέρᾳ τῆς ἀναστάσεως, αὐτῷ τῷ ἐπουρανίῳ νυμφίῳ, προσφέροντας αὐτῷ πλείστους ἐν δόξῃ ὠφεληθέντας ἐκ τῆς ἡμῶν συμπαθείας, χάριτι καὶ φιλανθρωπίᾳ αὐτοῦ τοῦ μονογενοῦς υἱοῦ τοῦ Θεοῦ, μεθ' οὗ τῷ Πατρὶ δόξα, ἅμα τῷ Ἁγίῳ Πνεύματι, νῦν καὶ ἀεὶ, καὶ εἰς αἰῶνας. Ἀμήν.—
S. Io. Chrysost. de Anathemate, tom. i. pp. 691—696.

Preface.

GLI AMMONISCE QUEL SAGGIO A PARTE A PARTE
COME LA FÈ PAGANA E INCERTA E LEVE
E MAL SICURO PEGNO!

Gerusal. Lib. Cant. v. lxxviii.

IN these words of Godfrey's, the Protestant may read, pretty much, what the Roman Catholics say of him and of the Church Reformed to which it is his privilege to belong. But, let them say as they list, and wrangle as they like, it matters not,—and were our lives but as Catholic as the Church to which we belong, we might set all fear aside and rejoice for the consolation!

The intent of the annexed Manual is

to show, in a short and simple way, the antiquity of our Faith, and the novelties of Romanism. I may add that it has been drawn up unwillingly. In fact, nothing but a stern sense of duty could have induced me to address my Parishioners on such points. But, I would not have it said hereafter that the watchman had not warned them, lest more than self-reproach should fall upon me. Besides, it has been said by the enemy that none of our Diocesans' staff have opened their lips, or put themselves in the gap; this reproach also, though I am the least amongst the Clergy of the Diocese, and in no ways attached to the Cathedral band, I could wish to roll off; and therefore, as independent in position as thought,—(as his Lordship the Bishop of the Diocese well knows, for against the united efforts of the Ecclesiastical Commissioners for England to the contrary, single-handed in the contest, I rescued for West Tarring a considerable portion of the Rectorial Rent Charge they would have sacrificed to an unhallowed expediency,—masked by the Acts of Parliament by which they are regulated, and under cover of which they have deprived the poor of twenty pounds Doles *per annum*, paid from time immemorial, and the Schools, in these days of Educational inquiry, of ten pounds *per annum* [1])—I have set my shoulder to the

---

[1] I speak these words with as much regret as truthfulness, because I am well aware that the time is not far off when Episcopal Revenues will be pared down to the quick ; and although none more than myself would regret such a course, yet many will conclude it a righteous retribution for timidity, and vacillating conduct, and the *seeming* desertion of their clergy. It is time for any Prelates, if such there be that follow it, to give over the DALAI LAMA system, and to come out of their place !

And far, far am I, in making these remarks, from bringing a " railing accusation " against any. The rather,—as the resolute defender of Episcopacy from day to day, and known as such,—I give utterance to

work. And if any say it might have
been done better, I join hands with
them, and wish they had saved me the
trouble of doing indifferently. Withal,
I would remind them of those words of
Jerome, in his Preface to Hosea, now
lying open before me: "*Quidam in
eo se disertos arbitrantur et doctos, si
alieno operi detrahant, et non quid ipsi
possint, sed quid nos non possimus, diju-
dicent.*"

Tom. vi.
p. 51.

To write a long book is no hard
matter. My desire has been to write a
short and an intelligible one, and for
this purpose I have sifted and bolted my
collections of many years into as small a

sentiments, not profitable to myself, in a worldly point
of view, but profitable in the long run to my Brethren
the Clergy! How many Bishops have I known
whose every thought was devoted to good! Alive or
dead it is well with such! Under such chief Pastors
none would wish all preferment in the hands of
Government! They looked to the labourer, and his
reward was sure!

space as possible, consistent with clearness of statement. He spoke very much to the purpose who said—"We find by experience that a long Act of Parliament, or an indenture and covenant that is of great length, ends none, but causes many contentions; and when many things are defined, and definitions spun out into declarations, men believe less, and know nothing more." I hope I shall not lead the reader into maze, or error, or doubt, or misgiving.

Jer. Tayl. x. 474.

But here let me remark that in stating the corruptions of the Church of Rome, I have never forgotten that the time was when the Papal power, raised and supported wholly by opinion, "with all its errors, its corruptions, and its crimes, was morally and intellectually the Conservative power of Christendom." A Church, but an erring Church, is the Church of Rome,—a brother and a sister still, though plunged in the mys-

Southey, Book of the Church, c. x. vol. i. 284.

tery of wickedness and a wanderer! The remark is Southey's, and always to be remembered; and I heartily wish that, at the present time, that tenth chapter of the "Book of the Church" were printed separately for distribution, which details the VIEW OF THE PAPAL SYSTEM. That chapter, and the ninth chapter of his "Life of Wesley," on the STATE OF RELIGION IN ENGLAND, contain more valuable and truthful matter than is readily found elsewhere.

At the same time that I speak thus fairly of the Papal Dominion and of the Roman Catholics, I wish to arouse all my readers to the fact, that Supremacy is never let out of her grasp—"SECULAR POWER, THOUGH FEIGNING STILL TO ACT BY SPIRITUAL," is her constant object! And it is to this inordinate desire to sway the consciences of her votaries that I attribute chiefly the recent ill-judged step which has roused this country as

Par. Lost,
xii. 517.

one man. And even now, as I write these lines, the evidence of the influence that Roman Catholics can bring to bear upon the young and upon the old is instanced in two reports in the *Times* newspaper — the one that of MISS TALBOT, the other that of poor MATHURIN CARRÉ. Let us be warned in time, and submit to no such tyrannical domination!

"And now, since no wise man will ever suspect us, that we will ever grow to that height of madness as to run perfidiously from the standard of God to the tents of the Roman Antichrist,—is there any hope that the Papists will ever be drawn back to the sound and pure judgment of the Primitive Antiquity? Oh! that God would vouchsafe this grace to the Christian world, that we could but comfort ourselves with the hope of so great happiness!" Bp. HALL, "No Peace with Rome," vol. i. 683. Folio.

As an instance of our regard for that reverend antiquity which the Papists appeal to and abuse, I have given numerous extracts from the Fathers as introductions to each Sermon. It will not detract from the value of my own collections to state, that Jewel has used very many of them. I detected this in recently going over his works, when preparing the Life of that worthy, inserted in a recent number of the *English Review,* and in which I have spoken of his fair fame in terms of deserved veneration, respect, and admiration.

I will only add in words from Bishop Croft's " Legacy "—" No man is such a stranger in our Jerusalem as not to know what is daily discoursed in all places. Many timorous zealots cannot hold in their fears; many insulting Papists cannot hold in their hopes that Popery will again bear rule in this nation. For my own part, weighing

things according to reason, I mean such
reason as God hath given one, I cannot
see any great probability of it."

Ed. 1679,
4to, p. 68

VICARAGE, WEST TARRING, SUSSEX,
April 14, 1851.

" In ipsâ item Catholicâ Ecclesiâ magnoperè curandum est, ut id teneamus, *quod ubique, quod semper, quod ab omnibus*, creditum est : (Hoc est etenim verè propriéque Catholicum, quod, ipsa vis nominis ratioque declarat, quæ omnia ferè universaliter comprehendit,) sed hoc ita demum fiet ; si sequamur *Universitatem, Antiquitatem, Consensionem.* Sequemur autem *Universitatem* hoc modo, si hanc unam fidem veram esse fateamur, quam tota per orbem terrarum confitetur Ecclesia : *Antiquitatem* verò ita, si ab his sensibus nullatenus recedamus, quos sanctos majores ac Patres nostros celebrâsse manifestum est : *Consensionem* quoque itidem : si in ipsâ vetustate, omnium vel certè pene omnium Sacerdotum pariter et Magistrorum definitiones sententiasque sectemur." — VINCENT. LIRIN. *adv. Hæreses*, c. ii.

" Ille est verus, et germanus Catholicus, qui veritatem Dei, qui Ecclesiam, qui Christi corpus diligit, qui divinæ religioni, qui Catholicæ fidei nihil præponit ; non hominis cujuspiam auctoritatem, non amorem, non ingenium, non eloquentiam, non philosophiam ; sed hæc cuncta despiciens, et in fide fixus, et stabilis permanens, quidquid universaliter antiquitùs Ecclesiam Catholicam tenuisse cognoverit, id solum tibi tenendum credendumque decernit : quidquid vero ab aliquo deinceps uno, præter omnes, vel contra omnes Sanctos novum et inauditum subinduci senserit, id non ad religionem, sed ad tentationem potius intelligat pertinere."—IBID. c. xx.

CONTENTS.

SERMON I.

THE SCRIPTURES.

2 Tim. iii. 16, 17.

SERMON II.

PART I.

THE CHURCH.

Acts ii. 4.

a

SERMON V.

CONFESSION AND ABSOLUTION.——THE DOCTRINE
OF THE CHURCH AND THE ERRORS OF ROME.

PROV. xxviii. 13.

SERMON VI.

PART I.

THE FAITH ONCE DELIVERED UNTO THE
SAINTS.

JUDE ver. 3.

SERMON VI.

PART II.

" ARE WE BLIND ALSO ? "

JOHN ix. 40, 41.

" Trust not their church with her scope infinite,
  As king-ships in this world, more in the other ;
  Here to seem greater than refined right,
  There both of grace and innocence a mother ;
    For God, a pope ; for angels, cardinals ;
    A church more overbuilt than Babel's walls.

          .   .   .   .   .   .

" Suffer not men of this divine profession
  Which should be great within, religious, true,
  As heralds sent by God to work progression
  From sin, to grace, and make the old man new ;
    Let them not with the world's moralities,
    Think to hold up their doctrine with the wise.

" Let them not fall into the common moulds
  Of frail humanity, which scandal give ;
  From God they must take notice what they should ;
  Men watch not what they speak, but how they live.
    Malice soon pierceth pomp's mortality,
    The sin derides her own hypocrisie.

" The clergies' praise, when they from pulpit come,
  Is to keep that decorum in their lives,
  Which wall them in, from each unreverend doom
  Of libertines, who to deface them strive ;
    For messengers of heaven must still appear,
    As if that heaven, not earth, were to them dear."

        LORD BROOKE, *A Treatise of Monarchie*. SECT. xiii.

SERMON I.

THE SCRIPTURES.

"Divinas Scripturas sæpius lege, immò nunquam de manibus tuis sacra lectio deponatur."—HIEROM. *Ep.* lii. *ad Nepot.* tom. i. 259.   Ed. Ver.

"Omni studio legendæ nobis Scripturæ sunt, et in lege Domini meditandum die ac nocte : ut probati trapezitæ, sciamus quis nummus probus sit, quis adulter."—IBID. *in Ephes.* lib. iii. c. v. tom. vii. p. 637.

Πᾶσα γραφὴ Θεόπνευστος καὶ ὠφέλιμος, διὰ τοῦτο συγγραφεῖσα παρὰ τοῦ Πνεύματος, ἵν' ὥσπερ ἐν κοινῷ τῶν ψυχῶν ἰατρείῳ, πάντες ἄνθρωποι τὸ ἴαμα τοῦ οἰκείου πάθους ἕκαστος ἐκλεγώμεθα.—BASIL. *in Psalm.* i. tom. i. p. 90.   Paris, 1722.

Μηδὲ περιμείνῃς ἕτερον διδάσκαλον· ἔχεις τὰ λόγια τοῦ Θεοῦ, οὐδείς σε διδάσκει ὡς ἐκεῖνα ·—Ἀκούσατε, παρακαλῶ, πάντες οἱ βιωτικοὶ, καὶ κτᾶσθε βιβλία φάρμακα τῆς ψυχῆς· εἰ μηδὲν ἕτερον βούλεσθε, τὴν γοῦν καινὴν κτήσασθε, τῶν ἀποστόλων τὰς πράξεις, τὰ εὐαγγέλια, διδασκάλους διηνεκεῖς.—Τοῦτο πάντων αἴτιον τῶν κακῶν, τὸ μὴ εἰδέναι τὰς γραφάς.—CHRYSOST. *Hom.* ix. *in Coloss.* tom. xi. 391.

" In his *omnibus* libris timentes Deum et pietate mansueti, quærunt voluntatem Dei.   Cujus operis et laboris prima observatio est, ut diximus, *nosse* istos libros," &c. &c.—AUGUST. *de Doctr. Christ.* lib. ii. 14, tom. iii. 24.

" Modus autem ipse dicendi, quo Sancta Scriptura contexitur, quàm omnibus accessibilis, quamvis paucissimis penetrabilis.   Ea quæ aperta continet, quasi amicus familiaris, sine fuco ad cor loquitur indoctorum atque doctorum."—AUGUST. *Epist.* iii. *ad Volusian.* tom. ii. 409.

SERMON I.

THE SCRIPTURES.

2 TIM. iii. 16, 17.

" All Scripture is given by inspiration of God, and is
profitable for doctrine, for reproof, for correction,
for instruction in righteousness; that the man of
God may be perfect, throughly furnished unto all
good works."

MANY a time and oft, Christian Brethren,
within the last seventeen years, have I
addressed you in these Holy Words from
this place, and have shown you, as the
Angel said to Daniel, the man of desires
and greatly beloved, *" that which is noted
in the Scripture of truth."* And, once Dan. x. 21.
more, am I called to speak boldly, as I
ought to speak, and herein to assure you,

B 2

that "*whatsoever things were written afore-time were written for our learning, that we through patience and comfort of the Scrip-*Rom. xv. 4. *tures might have hope.*"

And great cause there is that I should do so, my Brethren greatly beloved,——ye amongst whom, in trouble and in joy, I have gone in and out these many years! For once more hath the Church of Rome awoke out of her pretended sleep, and, like Samson of old time, hath "*said, I will go out as at other times before, and* Judg. xvi. *shake myself.*" And shook herself she 20. hath, and become intrusive; and us too would she shake, were the word of the Lord departed from us! Ay, had she the power, as she hath the will, she would hinder free access to the Book of Life, which is the BIBLE—that HOLY BOOK which is the hope and the stay, the solace and the comfort, of all those who love the Lord Jesus in sincerity, and look to Him, and Him alone, in faith and hope, rejoicing in a name that *pro-testeth* against error and cleaveth unto the truth!

Then, that your hearts and minds may continue grounded and settled in a true belief, and in communion with that pure and apostolical branch of Christ's Holy Catholic Church established in these kingdoms, and, as such, directly opposed to Romish or other corruptions, I purpose, by God's help, in this and some following Discourses, to call your attention to that Faith in which ye stand. And if, in so doing, I have to go a little out of my common way, which is to speak of "*Christ and him crucified*" only,—of a holy faith and a holy life, and of things accompanying salvation,— ye must pardon me in this matter, considering that a sort of "*necessity is laid upon me*," and that my very and only object is, as I did promise when ordained Priest, "with all faithful diligence to banish and drive away all erroneous and strange doctrines contrary to God's word," using for that cause "both public and private monitions and exhortations."

1 Cor. ix. 16.

Ord. of Priests.

These remarks thrown out, I proceed

at once to a consideration of the Holy Scriptures, all-sufficient [1], as we do think and profess, for salvation,—noting merely, by the way, that we, who protest against the errors of Rome, take not up that notion of the Puritan platform, that "Scripture is the only rule of all things which in this life may be done by men;" that it "must be the rule to direct in all things, even so far as to the taking up of a rush or straw." Far from this: and the discussion of this matter, which, as

Hooker, Ecc. Pol. ii. i. § 2.

---

[1] "Scripture complains justly of these main wrongs offered to it :—The first, of addition to the Canon ; the second, of the detraction from the sufficiency of it ; the third, of hanging all the authority thereof upon the sleeve of Rome."—Bp. Hall, "*No Peace with Rome*," vol. i. 673, folio. But hear the words of St. Chrysostom : Μετὰ πολλῆς σπουδῆς τὴν ἀνάγνωσιν τῶν θείων γραφῶν ποιώμεθα· οὕτω γὰρ καὶ τῆς γνώσεως ἐπιτευξόμεθα, εἰ συνεχῶς ἐπίωμεν τὰ ἐγκείμενα· οὐδὲ γάρ ἐστι τὸν μετὰ σπουδῆς καὶ πολλοῦ πόθου τοῖς θείοις ἐντυγχάνοντα περιοφθῆναί ποτε· ἀλλὰ κἂν ἄνθρωπος ἡμῖν μὴ γένηται διδάσκαλος, αὐτὸς ὁ δεσπότης ἄνωθεν ἐμβατεύων ταῖς καρδίαις ἡμετέραις φωτίζει τὴν διάνοιαν, καταυγάζει τὸν λογισμόν, ἐκκαλύπτει τὰ λανθάνοντα, διδάσκαλος ἡμῖν γίνεται τῶν ἀγνοουμένων· μόνον ἐὰν ἡμεῖς τὰ παρ' ἑαυτῶν εἰσφέρειν βουλώμεθα.—*In Gen. Hom.* xxxv. tom. iv. 351.

extremes meet, will again arise, we leave in the glowing pages of the judicious HOOKER. But what we assert and maintain is this, in the words of our sixth Article, that " Holy Scripture containeth all things necessary to salvation : so that whatsoever is not read therein, nor may be proved thereby, is not to be required of any man, that it should be believed as an Article of the Faith, or be thought requisite or necessary to salvation." In this, and in this sense alone, is it asserted that THE BIBLE AND THE BIBLE ONLY is the religion of Protestants. And hence it is that, in the Ordering of Priests, or ever they be sent forth to preach all saving truths, this question is put, " Are you persuaded that the Holy Scriptures contain sufficiently all doctrine required of necessity for eternal salvation, through faith in Jesus Christ ? and are you determined, out of the said Scriptures, to instruct the people committed to your charge, and to teach nothing, as required of necessity to eternal salvation, but that which you shall be persuaded may be concluded and proved by the Scripture?" And the answer is, "I am so persuaded, and have so determined by God's grace." In other words, the Scripture is our CANON or RULE of Faith. Than it, other we do want none; and we do apply the words of the text (not stopping to inquire whether necessarily[2] so applied at first or not) to those "canonical books of the Old and New Testament, of whose authority was never any doubt in the

Art. VI.
Church." Simply expressive these words are, and enough they are for us, who are

Isa. xxxv. 8.
plain "*wayfaring men,*" on our journey to the heavenly Canaan. "*All Scripture is given by inspiration of God, and is profitable for doctrine, for reproof, for correction, for instruction in righteousness:*

---

[2] See Theophylact in loc. "Ποία; περὶ ἧς διελέγετο, περὶ ἧς εἶπεν ὅτι ἱερά."—Tom. ii. 612. He collects the general statement. Hooker refers (as does Allestree, ii. 5.) the ἱερὰ γράμματα to the Old Testament.—Eccl. Pol. i. xiv. 4. Jeremy Taylor, to the Old and New, as this Epistle was written "certainly after three of the Gospels."—Vol. x. 270. For the Inspiration, see Secker's Serm. vol. vi. 84.

that the man of God may be perfect,
throughly furnished unto all good works."
Such is God's word, and so we believe.

And here it is, Christian Brethren, that,
as regards the Scripture of truth, ourselves and they of the Church of Rome
differ. As that holy and humble-minded
man of heart said, in the Country Parson;
Unto the Protestant, " the chief and top
of his knowledge consists in the Book
of Books, the storehouse and magazine
of life and comfort, the Holy Scrip- George
tures. There he sucks and lives." Not Count. Parson, c. iv.
so the Romanist, who declares his Rule
of Faith to be contained partly in WRIT-
TEN BOOKS, and partly in UNWRITTEN
TRADITIONS, which are to be received
" with sentiments of equal piety and
reverence[3] ;" numbering amongst the

---

[3] The passages referred to are, " Perspiciensque hanc
veritatem et disciplinam contineri in libris scriptis, et
sine scripto Traditionibus, &c.—pari pietatis affectu ac
reverentiâ suscipit, et veneratur." And the con-
cluding words are, " Si quis autem libros ipsos integros
cum omnibus suis partibus, prout in Ecclesiâ Catholicâ
legi consueverunt, et in veteri vulgatâ Latinâ editione
habentur, pro·sacris et Canonicis non susceperit, et

written Books those Books of the Apocrypha which (as Hierome saith) "the Church doth read for example of life and instruction of manners; but yet doth it not apply them to establish any doctrine:" none of them being referred to in the New Testament, "*the book of the generation of Jesus Christ.*" And yet, as concerns these Books, and the aforenamed Traditions also, the decree of the Church of Rome is this: "If any one shall not receive these entire Books with all their parts as sacred and canonical, just as they have been wont to be read in the Catholic (*i. e.* Roman) Church, and in the old common Latin edition, and shall wittingly and wilfully despise the aforesaid Traditions, let him be accursed." Such are the words decreed in the Fourth Session of Trent, the 8th day of April, 1546; and against these and like words

Art. VI.

Matt. i. 1.

traditiones prædictas sciens et prudens contempserit; Anathema sit."

Those who would pursue the subject must consult Bellarmine, who states " Totalis regula Fidei est Verbum Dei, sive revelatio Dei Ecclesiæ facta, quæ dividitur in duas regulas partiales, Scripturam et Traditionem," &c.—*De Verbo Dei*, lib. iv. c. 12.

is our Article framed, even as originally published in 1552, thus declaring, in opposition to the Romanists, our full and entire belief in Holy Scripture only.

And, not to darken counsel with words, Job xxxviii. 2. and to trouble you with matters of discussion on such a point, it will be enough to say, that herein is a vast difference—a great gulph fixed between the Romanists and ourselves. As one says well, "If the Bible is the sole fountain of Christian faith to the Church of England, and *not* the sole fountain of Christian faith to the Church of Rome, the authority admitted by the latter, *in addition* to the authority of the Bible, must constitute an essential difference between the two churches[4]." And even so it is, and the difference must continue as long as

[4] See Bp. Marsh's Comparative View of the Churches of England and Rome, c. i. p. 3, 1st edition. A book very much to be recommended. He remarks below, " The subject of Tradition, which to the Church of Rome is a Rule of Faith, however intelligible it may be thought by those who have not examined it in all its bearings, is really one of the most *intricate* subjects in dogmatic theology."—Ibid. p. 9.

the cause of difference exists. But, in such a discourse as this, I do not think it necessary to enter further on the difficult subject of Tradition, as hampered by the Romanist. Therefore, I will only add, that you must not confound the "Traditions and Ceremonies" mentioned in our thirty-fourth Article, which mean only Customs and Directions[5], with those Traditions which the Church of Rome holds to be *Divine* and *Apostolic*, and a rule of faith to them, even as the Holy Scriptures, our joy and our glory, are to us. To the Bible alone we do hold for truth. Touching Traditions, in the Romish approved sense, such as have a correspondence with, or an attestation from the written Word, these are well enough in their way, and are received by us for as much as they are worth ; for the rest, as one said, we justly disclaim them "as unworthy to appear upon that awful bench, amongst the inspired Penmen of God."

See Bp. Hall, "The Old Religion," c. xvi. § 39.

[5] Any discussion on the παραδόσεις in 2 Thess. ii. 15, would come under this head.

But, although I do not think it necessary to proceed, as I said, in a discussion
of this sort, ill suited to general apprehension, yet must I warn you that from
Tradition, as upheld by the Church of
Rome, some of her chiefest errors—I
might say all of them—have arisen.
These will be noted in due course, as the
subjects pass in review before us. What,
however, I would for the present direct
your attention to, is the fact, that the
Church of Rome permits the use only of
one authorized Version, whether translated or not,—that is to say, the Old
Vulgate; and from this, if she can establish a doctrine, as more than one she
doth, no appeal is allowed; whereas in
the Church to which we are privileged
to belong, though we have a translation
(one of the best ever made) "appointed
to be read in Churches," yet for all that
we are not debarred from the use of the
inspired originals, whether in the Hebrew
or the Greek[6]. Such as can use them,

[6] This, though not expressed in so many words in
our Formularies, is inferred from the *Reformatio Legum*

may, and derive comfort, as many do, whilst searching for hidden treasure. Beyond a doubt, with the originals at hand, or such a translation as we have, there is no palming, even upon the most ignorant, what are called in our First Homily " the stinking puddles of men's Traditions, devised by man's imaginations, for our justification and salvation." It was, in fact, by prohibiting, or, to say the least, by so restricting the use of Holy Writ as to amount to a prohibition, that corruption gained ground in the Church of Rome,—such corruption as almost to overwhelm her,—so that the wisest and the best of her own sons called out for redress, and called long in vain. Yea, even to this day, though in some sort the restriction on the reading of the Bible has been relaxed as regards the

Ecclesiasticarum. See " *De Summâ Trinitate et Fide Catholicâ*," cap. 12. " Cæterum in lectione divinarum Scripturarum si qua occurrerint ambigua vel obscura in veteri Testamento, eorum interpretatio ex fonte Hebraicæ veritatis petatur, in novo autem Græci codices consulantur." We have to thank Dr. Cardwell for a new and useful reprint.

Romanists of *our own country*, yet has it been unwillingly and grudgingly; and elsewhere the veil has not been lifted up, but the covering remains, and God's own book is almost a sealed one. Once upon a time[7] it was said, "more harm than good arose from an indiscriminate use of the Scriptures in the vulgar tongue," and none was to possess them without a licence from the Bishop or Inquisitor, and that on the representation of the Priest or Confessor—and no bookseller was allowed to sell them. Happily, as intimated, this is no longer tolerated here. This land of liberty shook off *that* yoke! Lands, however, there are, Christian Brethren, and those no distant ones, in which the Bible yet, to all practical intents and purposes, is unread by the people. And if, where the

---

[7] " Cum experimento manifestum sit, si sacra Biblia vulgari linguâ passim sive discrimine permittantur, *plus inde*, ob hominum temeritatem, *detrimenti quam utilitatis oriri*," &c. Reg. iv.

De libris Prohibitis Regulæ per Patres à Tridentinâ Synodo delectos concinnatæ, et a Pio PP. comprobatæ.

Romanists have their own translation,—
as they have in this country,—corruptions flourish and abound, even as they
do, upheld by Tradition, what must be
the case in those lands where the dimness is as it was, and no light shines, and
the people walk in darkness—not knowing, because they search not the Scriptures?

And I have put the matter in this,
the most favourable, light, because, did
you say to a Romanist that the use of
the Scriptures was denied to the people,
he would contradict you flatly; whereas,
all the while, it is only an authorized
and corrupted Version that is permitted
to those unto whom it is permitted,
whilst unto the multitude the understanding of the Scriptures is pretty much
as it ever was.   In a word, it is not en-
couraged.   They are consigned over to
the priesthood, who, by this means, bear
sway, and lord it over weak consciences,
prescribing Tradition for what has no
other proof.   And therefore the very
commencing sentences of our Homilies

speak clearly to the purpose, not allowing the people to be deceived. "Unto a Christian man there can be nothing either more necessary or profitable than the knowledge of Holy Scripture ; forasmuch as in it is contained God's true word, setting forth His glory, and also man's duty. And there is no truth nor doctrine necessary for our justification and everlasting salvation, but that is, or may be, drawn out of that fountain and well of truth." Certain sure, as that ancient Father said, calling to mind our Saviour's words, "Ignorance of the Scriptures is ignorance of Christ [8]."

But, and if any should argue still for the use of Tradition, and say, A time there was when all was not written that concerns our everlasting salvation [9],—at

[8] The words are St. Jerome's : " Ignoratio Scripturarum ignoratio Christi est." Prolog. in Isaiam. They are referred to in our Homily on " The Information of certain places of the Scripture," Part I. Professor Corrie's edition, with all quotations verified, is much to be recommended.

[9] This point is clearly put by Bp. Kaye, in his Lectures on Tertullian, who remarked thus, in 1825 : " If we mistake not the signs of the times, the period is

once we admit it.   But then, bear in mind, my Christian Brethren, that at that time, and till all was written that should be written, there was a "Spirit of Infallible Record put into the Apostles sufficient for its publication;" and, since then, infallibility hath passed away from the earth.   Yea, though Rome do claim it, asserting herself to be "of all Churches the mother and the mistress," yet is it a word only, and beyond that nothing !

Truly, that the Scriptures are enough for us, and all we need, the God of our salvation hath Himself declared; for generally applicable are those His words to the Sadducees : " *Ye do err, not knowing the Scriptures.*"   And, were even a more decided abnegation of Tradition necessary, considerable is it what St. John says : " *Many other signs truly did Jesus in the presence of His disciples, which are*

Jer. Tayl. x. 389.

Conc. Trid. sess. vii. can. iii. De Baptismo.

Matt. xxii. 29.

not far distant when the whole controversy between the English and Romish Churches will be revived," &c. p. 299, 2nd edit.   See Southey's " Colloquies," vol. ii. p. 414.

not written in this Book: but these are written, that ye might believe that Jesus is the Christ, the Son of God; and that believing ye might have life through His name[10]." To the like intent also were John xx. 30, 31. St. Luke's words. Write would he unto the *"most excellent Theophilus,"* and write in order, what appertained unto Christ's sojourn as a man amongst men. And why? *"That thou mightest know the certainty of those things, wherein thou hast been instructed."* And what did St. Luke i. 4. Paul, when, at Thessalonica, he would convince the synagogue of the Jews? Turned he, think you, to the Traditions

[10] " If it be said that this place must be understood of Christ's miracles only ; I answer, that miracles without the doctrine of Christ, and knowledge of His sufferings, can bring no man to life everlasting ; and therefore the place must be understood of the doctrine of Christ, and not of His miracles alone," &c. &c. This extract is from a Treatise well worth reprinting, W. Perkins's " REFORMED CATHOLIC ; or, a Declaration, showing how near we may come to the present Church of Rome in sundry points of Religion, and wherein we must for ever depart from them." Vol. i. p. 574, folio, 1608. It is, however, to be noted, that he was a rigid Predestinarian, and that he denied Rome to be a Church at all,—which we do not, neither do our Articles.

of their law, which had subverted that law, and made " *the commandment of God* Matt. xv. 6. *of none effect?*" Not so! But, "*as his manner was,*" he "*went in unto them, and three Sabbath days reasoned with them out of the Scriptures, opening and alledging, that Christ must needs have suffered,* Acts xvii. 2, 3. *and risen again from the dead.*" From which, and from other numerous passages, it is quite clear that the written word, without unwritten Tradition [11], is enough for us men, and for our salvation. We need no safer nor better argument than this. So it is written, and so we believe!

Whereto, be it added, that this was the will of God concerning us from the first. For, when Moses recapitulated the Law, he said, what is also said in Rev. xxii. 18, 19. the summing up of the New Testament, "*Ye shall not add unto the word which I command you, neither shall ye diminish*

[11] The words of Jerome on Haggai, c. i. 11, are much to be remembered words : " Sed et alia quæ absque auctoritate et testimoniis Scripturarum quasi traditione Apostolicâ sponte reperiunt atque confingunt, percutit gladius Dei." Tom. vi. 749, E.

*ought from it, that ye may keep the com-
mandments of the Lord your God which
I command you.*" And then, within a _{Deut. iv. 2.}
chapter or two, occur these and other
like words also, "*These words, which I
command thee this day, shall be in thine
heart: and thou shalt teach them diligently
unto thy children, and shalt talk of them
when thou sittest in thine house, and when
thou walkest by the way, and when thou
liest down, and when thou risest up.*" So Deut. vi.
6, 7.
spake God of old time by Moses, the
meekest of His servants. And "*when
the fulness of the time was come,*" and Gal. iv. 4.
God was manifest in the flesh, other
none were these His sacred words,
(equally significant, however understood,)
" SEARCH THE SCRIPTURES; *for in them
ye think ye have eternal life: and they
are they which testify of me.*" And this John v. 39.
it was which turned to the praise of the
Beræans, "*that they received the word
with all readiness of mind,* AND SEARCHED
THE SCRIPTURES *daily, whether those
things were so.*" And so also was the Acts xvii.
11.
ignorance of Candace's eunuch enlight-

Acts viii. 27.

ened. As he journeyed he read the truth, and the great and good God took care that his reading and his search chap. viii. should not be in vain. Yea, "*the Spirit*" spake unto Philip, and Philip, taught of God, instructed this chamberlain in the truth, and that truth made him free; and, in finding Christ of whom Isa. lvi. 5. Esaias spake in that marvellous chapter, he gained unto himself "*a name better than of sons and of daughters : an everlasting name, that shall not be cut off.*"

But, notwithstanding all these clear testimonies out of God's own word, it was said, in our earlier disputes with the Romanists: "It is not thought good—to let every curious busybody of the vulgar sort read and examine the Bible in their common language;" and again, it was "the saucy malapertness of heretics [12],"

[12] These are the words of Harding to which Jewel severally replies. See vol. iii. 282, and vol. vi. 202. Scarce any armoury is like to Jewel's for materials against the Romanist. Unanswered and unanswerable are his Treatises ! I may be allowed here to refer to his Life in No. xxviii. of the Eng. Rev., in which I trust I have so made mention of a venerable worthy as not to tarnish his fair fame.

(that is, Protestants,) which forced the governors of the Church to limit their reading. In which, and in like words at any time uttered, put no trust, ye Christian people! They are but vain words, and used merely to deter you from reading those Scriptures which are able to make you "*wise unto salvation through faith which is in Christ Jesus.*" Open unto you they are every whit. In a tongue "understanded of the people," they were set forth as soon as might be, as were also the Services of our Church. With us there was no muffling up in a strange language, nor mumbling in an unknown speech! The great things of salvation were at once thrown open, even as God willed they should be. And if there were some things "*hard to be understood* [13]," those also, if necessary, in His own good time, God would take care to reveal. Men might shut, but He would open!

2 Tim. iii. 15.

Art. XXIV.

2 Pet. iii. 16. τίνα δυσνόητα.

---

[13] See Abp. Potter's "Prælectiones Theologicæ," Præl. xx. p. 306. These may safely be referred to as a whole. They take for their text 2 Tim. iii. 16, 17.

Then again, because formerly books were rare, and many (even as now), if they had them, could not read them, *their* case also was looked to, not only in the public preaching of the Scriptures, but in that short summary of the Faith, called the Apostles' Creed. So that when a man had no opportunity of knowing more, to him the Bible was briefly summed up in some such words as these: "*He that believeth on the Son of God hath the witness in himself.*" "*This is life eternal that they might know Thee the only true God, and Jesus Christ, whom Thou hast sent.*" Such knowledge was very good. It appertained unto salvation. And this Creed was not set forth as the word of God itself, or as " a suppletory to deficiencies of Scripture;" but simply as a short summary of that word which God had spoken—which same word, as Christ said unto the Jews, shall "*judge*" us "*in the last day.*"

1 John v. 10.

John xvii. 3.

Jer. Tayl. x. 384.

John xii. 48.

To say the truth, overmuch talk about the difficulties of Scripture is not wise[14].

[14] Very applicable here are Augustine's words.

WHAT THE LORD GOD INTENDED
SHOULD BE UNDERSTOOD OF ALL, THAT
HE WOULD TAKE CARE ALL SHOULD
UNDERSTAND. Difficulties, doubtless,
there are plenty in the Bible; but no
difficulties concerning salvation; and that
is the matter which concerns us; and
the old saying is true : " The lamb may
walk therein, and the elephant may
swim." As it has been declared from
the first by the old Fathers of the
Church, whose word we despise not
when it agrees with the Word of God [15],
all necessary portions of Scripture are
clear, plain, open, manifest. Matters
they are for thought and meditation, not
only in the Church and from the priest's

Adv. Julian. Pelag. lib. v. c. 2. " Exaggeras quàm
sit *difficilis, paucisque conveniens eruditis, sanctarum cog-
nitio literarum,*" &c. Tom. x. 627. The saying below
is from St. Gregory. It occurs in his Epistle to
Leander, prefixed to his Commentary on the Book of
Job, and is often quoted by Jewel. E. g. ii. 119, iii. 218.

[15] " We allow the ancient Fathers the same credit
that they themselves have ever desired," says Jewel,
referring to Augustine's words to Fortunatus. See
Defence of Apol., vol. iv. 184, and Dr. Jelf's Index
v. Fathers.

mouth, but the children with their fathers are to talk of the same—yea, the smiths, the artificers, the labourers, the sempsters—the very ditchers, the gardeners, and the cowherds [16], as well as the doctors of the Church—have capacity to comprehend them. Oftentimes, indeed, the unlearned see farther than the learned, and things hidden from "*the wise and prudent*" are "*revealed unto babes.*" Christ Himself hath willed it, that humbleness of mind, meekness, and lowly diligence, should have spiritual discernment, when blindness in part falls upon the high-minded. Therefore, away

Matt. xi. 25.

[16] The passage here alluded to, is that well-known one of Theodoret : " Καὶ ἔστιν ἰδεῖν ταῦτα εἰδότας τὰ δόγματα, οὐ μόνους γε τῆς ἐκκλησίας τοὺς διδασκάλους, ἀλλὰ καὶ σκυτοτόμους καὶ χαλκοτύπους καὶ ταλασιουργοὺς, καὶ τοὺς ἄλλους ἀποχειροβιώτους· καὶ γυναῖκας ὡσαύτως, οὐ μόνον τὰς λόγων μετεσχηκυίας, ἀλλὰ καὶ χερνήτιδας καὶ ἀκεστρίας, καὶ μέντοι καὶ θεραπαίνας· καὶ οὐ μόνον αὐτοὶ, ἀλλὰ καὶ χωρικοὶ τήνδε τὴν γνῶσιν ἐσχήκασι· καὶ ἔστιν εὑρεῖν καὶ σκαπανέας καὶ βοηλάτας καὶ φυτουργοὺς περὶ τῆς θείας διαλεγομένους Τριάδος, καὶ περὶ τῆς τῶν ὅλων δημιουργίας, καὶ τὴν ἀνθρωπείαν φύσιν εἰδότας Ἀριστοτέλους πολλῷ μᾶλλον καὶ Πλάτωνος." Græc. Affect. Curat. lib. v. Περὶ Φύσεως Ἀνθρώπου, p. 220. *Ed. Gaisford.*

with all else, as necessary and of equal import with Scripture! Away with Traditions and man's devices! To the Gospel of Jesus Christ; *"to the law and to the testimony: if they speak not according to this word, it is because there is no light in them."* Away with all needless enumeration of difficulties; for those of one place are made clear in another [17]. THE BIBLE — THE BIBLE WORD, that is your treasure—the treasure of all the baptized, ye Christian People! "Let every man, woman, and child, therefore, with all their heart, thirst and desire God's Holy Scriptures; love them; embrace them; have their delight and pleasure in hearing and reading them; so as at length we may be transformed and changed into them.

Isa. viii. 20.

[17] So August.: "In iis enim quæ apertè in Scripturis posita sunt inveniuntur illa omnia quæ continent fidem moresque vivendi, spem scilicet atque caritatem." De Doctr. Christ. lib. ii. c. ix. tom. iii. 24, and the words of Epiphanius are, on this point, generally applicable: Πάντα ἡμῖν φωτεινὰ τὰ τῆς θείας γραφῆς, καὶ τὰ τῆς ἁγίας πίστεως, καὶ οὐδὲν σκολιὸν, ἢ ἐναντίον ἢ στραγγαλιῶδες.—ANOMÆI HÆRESIS, lxxvi. CONFUTATIO xxviii. tom. i. 975, D. Ed. 1622.

For the Holy Scriptures are God's treasure-house, wherein are found all things needful for us to see, to hear, to learn, and to believe, necessary for the attaining eternal life." Yea, hath not God said : *"My Spirit that is upon thee, and my words which I have put in thy mouth, shall not depart out of thy mouth, nor out of the mouth of thy seed, nor out of the mouth of thy seed's seed, saith the Lord, from henceforth and for ever ?"* Good words and comfortable words these, I trow, ye Christian People! Hold to them, and inherit a blessing!

Of the Information of Certain Places of the Scripture, 1st Part.

Isa. lix. 21.

And thus, as far as the Scriptures are concerned, having dwelt upon the distinguishing marks between ourselves and the Romanists, I will conclude by a short reference to the text, premising first, in the words of the Proverbs, *"Every word of God is pure: He is a shield unto them that put their trust in Him. Add thou not unto His words, lest He reprove thee, and thou be found a liar."*

Prov. xxx. 5, 6.

I. And the topping consideration is,

Christian Brethren, that "*all Scripture*"—the whole of the Scripture—"*is given by inspiration of God.*" As at the first He breathed into man's nostrils the breath of life, and so man became a living soul, thus also breathed He into this Holy Book the Spirit of Life, and "*holy men of God spake*"—not their own words—but "*as they were moved by the Holy Ghost.*" The dictation is none of theirs', but God's. All-sacred is the BOOK OF BOOKS, penned by no human device, but Heaven-descended, and glorious altogether, the Old as well as the New Testament. "The difference between them consisting in this, that the Old did make wise by teaching salvation through Christ that should come; the New, by teaching that Christ the Saviour is come, and that Jesus whom the Jews did crucify, and whom God did raise again from the dead, is He." "*To Him give all the prophets witness, that through His name whosoever believeth in Him shall receive remission of sins.*" Such is the Bible, stamped with the impress of the Almighty. On

2 Pet. i. 21.

Hooker's E. P. i. xiv. 4.

Acts x. 43.

it the teeth of time[18] have no power, neither can Tradition choke it, nor the fire consume it, nor man gainsay it. Despite the wickedness of the wicked, "*the word of the Lord*" will *have free course, and be glorified.*" This and this alone is the standard and the beam to try the weights of truth and falsehood. As one saith, "The Holy Scriptures are the mercy-seat, the registry of the mysteries of God, our charter for the life to come, the holy place in which God showeth Himself to His people, the Mount Sion, where God hath appointed to dwell for ever."

2 Thess. iii. 1.

Jewell, Treatise of the Holy Scripture, Works, vol. vii. 293.

II. Next, the text declares them to be "*profitable for doctrine, for reproof, for correction, for instruction in righteousness;*" containing, that is, all that is needed for faith or practice [19]. As before

---

[18] " Men's works have an age like themselves ; and though they outlive their authors, yet have they a short period to their duration. This only is a work too hard for the teeth of time, and cannot perish but in the general flames, when all things shall confess their ashes."—Sir T. Brown, *Religio Medici,* § 23.

[19] " Ad utramque ergo partem utilis est Divina Scriptura, et ad partem intellectivam, et ad partem operativam."—Cajetan. in loc.

said, " Whatsoever is not read therein,
nor may be proved thereby, is not to be
required of any man that it should be
believed as an Article of the Faith, or
be thought requisite or necessary to sal- Art. VI.
vation." From them is to be derived all
doctrine; to them all doctrine is to be
referred. By them all wrong teaching
is convicted and reproved; by them the
truth is made manifest and clear when
it is judged. Overmatch is the Word,
as it comes from God, for the world, the
flesh and the devil. Before it, so to
say, " *Bel boweth down, Nebo stoopeth.*" Isa. xlvi. 1.
Stand they cannot, any more than Dagon
could, before the ark of God; for glori- 1 Sam. v. 3.
ous is the light of His truth, giving shine
unto the world. THE TRUTH AS IT IS
IN JESUS is there; and other truth than
that mortal man needeth not! From it
we learn—to it we defer—by it we are
saved! Otherwise turn we not, than to
" *the engrafted word which is able to save
our souls.*" It is even as the garner of James i. 21.
the Lord, and all good wheat is there.

And, *" What is the chaff to the wheat ? saith the Lord."*

Jer. xxiii. 28.

III. But, if the all-sacred Word be profitable for *" doctrine and reproof,"* so also is it *"for correction and instruction in righteousness."* As it is our RULE OF FAITH, so too is it our RULE OF PRACTICE. Certainly, if it was such to Timothy [20], it must be, even as it is, such unto us. And, verily, such an unbending rule man alway needeth ; for the corruption of his nature, and the naughtiness of his heart, are continually leading him to pervert the truth. And then it is that God speaketh unto him, by His Spirit, through his conscience oftentimes, and warneth him of what is written in the Book of Life ; *" and thine ears,"* thou Christian man, *" shall hear a word behind thee, saying, This is the way, walk ye in it, when ye turn to the right hand, and when ye turn to the left."* Ever doth

Isa. xxx. 21.

[20] So Chrysostom, Hom. ix. in loc., tom. xi. 714; Theophylact in loc., tom. ii. 612; and Œcumenius : Εἰ δὲ Τιμοθέῳ δεῖ ἀναγινώσκειν, πόσῳ μᾶλλον ἡμῖν ; tom. ii. p. 276, in loc.

God's Word give thee warning, with judgment correcting thy backslidings, summoning thee into the paths of Peace. Set on by God's piercing word, *" thine own wickedness shall correct thee, and thy backslidings shall reprove thee : know therefore and see that it is an evil thing and bitter, that thou hast forsaken the Lord thy God, and that my fear is not in thee, saith the Lord God of Hosts."* Jer. ii. 19.

IV. But and if, ye Christian people, correction is received, and instruction in righteousness cherished, and the word of the Lord is as *" a lantern unto our feet, and a light unto our path,"* and we re-ceive it, *" not as the word of men, but as it is in truth, the word of God, which effectually worketh also in you that be-lieve ;"* if we forsake not *" the fountain of living waters,"* nor hew us out *" cis-terns, broken cisterns, that can hold no water,"* but, on the contrary, drink living waters from that unsullied cistern of the Word of God; then, as sure as God's word is true, unto us shall come home that word which Christ, the living Word,

Ps. cxix. 105.

1 Thess. ii. 13.

Jer. ii. 13.

D

spake unto the woman of Samaria, "*Whosoever drinketh of the water that I shall give him shall never thirst; but the water that I shall give him shall be in him a well of water springing up unto everlast-*

John iv. 14; vi. 35.

ing life." And what then? "*Ho, every*

Isa. lv. 1.

one that thirsteth, come ye to the waters!" Thou "*man of God,*" or able minister,

Horbery, i. 136.

or pious Christian, that wouldest be "*perfect*" (after the short-comings of mortality), "*throughly furnished unto all good works,*" take thee this Holy Word in hand! For true, every whit, is that which David spake in the Spirit, "*The law of the Lord is an undefiled law, converting the soul; the testimony of the Lord is sure, and giveth wisdom unto the simple; the statutes of the Lord are right, and rejoice the heart; the commandment of the Lord is pure, and giveth light unto the eyes. The fear of the Lord is clean, and endureth for ever; the judgments of the*

Ps. xix. 7—9.

Lord are true and righteous altogether."

And thus, in these words of the text "be contained two arguments to prove the sufficiency of Scripture without unwritten verities. The first, that which is profitable to these four uses: namely, to teach all necessary truth, to confute all errors, to correct all faults in manners, and to instruct in righteousness, that is, to inform all men in all good duties, that are sufficient for salvation. Scripture serveth for all these uses, and therefore it is sufficient, and unwritten Traditions are superfluous. The second: that which can make the man of God, that is, Prophets, and Apostles, and Ministers of the Word, perfect in all the duties of their callings,—that same Word is sufficient to make all other men perfect in all good works[21]. But God's

[21] See Abp. Laud's summing up of "this long discourse to prove that Scripture is the Word of God," § xxxiv. Against Fisher the Jesuit, p. 85, &c. Ed. Cardwell. An old poet of our own, WARNER, in his Albion's England, has some very expressive lines on the all-sufficiency of Holy Scripture:

"Upon the onely Scripture doth our Church
　　Foundation lay；
Let Patriarchs, Prophets, Gospels, and th' Apostles for us say:
For soul and body we affirm are all-sufficient
　　they," &c. &c.—
　　　　Book ix. c. 52, p. 234. Ed. 4to, 1612.

Word is able to make the man of God

See
W. Per-
kins' "Re-
formed
Catholike,"
vol. i. 574.

perfect.   Therefore it is sufficient to
prescribe the true and perfect way to
eternal life, without the help of unwritten Traditions."

And now, Christian Brethren, when
all is said, this is the sum of all.   He
sent his Word and saved us!   First,
God's Incarnate Word died for us men
and for our salvation; and He, whose
providence ordereth all things aright,
caused holy men of old, as they were
moved by the Holy Ghost, to pen that
written Word which telleth unto us
men of that sacrifice once offered for
sin.   And as that sacrifice in itself, once
offered, is full and sufficient, "not only
for original guilt, but also for the actual

Art. II.

sins of men," so also is that Holy Word,
and He that speaketh by it.   "SEARCH

John v. 39.
Matt. xvii.
5.

THE SCRIPTURES."   "HEAR YE HIM[22]."

[22] The reader may be referred to the 5th volume
of Routh's Relliquiæ Sacræ for "*Testimonia de Authoritate S. Scripturæ Ante-Nicæna*," pp. 335—353.

SERMON II.

PART I.

THE CHURCH.

" Nolo humanis documentis, sed divinis oraculis Sanctam Ecclesiam demonstari."—AUGUST. *de Unitat. Eccles.* tom. ix. 341.

" Proinde sive de Christo, sive de ejus Ecclesiâ, sive de quâcunque aliâ re quæ pertinet ad fidem, vitamque nostram, non dicam nos, nequaquam comparandi ei qui dixit, ' Licet si nos,' sed omninò quod secutus adjecit, ' Si angelus de coelo vobis annuntiaverit præter quàm quod in Scripturis legalibus aut Evangelicis accepimus, Anathema sit.' "—IBID. *contr. Literas Petiliani*, lib. iii. 7, tom. ix. 301.

" Sola igitur Catholica Ecclesia est, quæ verum cultum retinet. Hic est fons veritatis; hoc est domicilium fidei; hoc templum Dei: quo si quis non intraverit, vel a quo si quis exiverit, a spe vitæ ac salutis æternæ alienus est."—LACTANT. *de Verâ Sapient.* lib. iv. c. 30.

" Et quare jubet in hoc tempore omnes Christianos conferre se ad Scripturas? Quia in tempore hoc, ex quo obtinuit hæresis illas Ecclesias, nulla probatio potest esse veræ Christianitatis, neque refugium potest esse Christianorum aliud, volentium cognoscere fidei veritatem, nisi Scripturæ divinæ."—CHRYSOST. (*ut ferunt*) *Opus Imp. in Matt. Hom.* xlix. tom. vi. cciv.

Ἐπειδὴ δὲ οὐκ αὐτοὶ μόνοι συνεπλήρουν τὸ σῶμα τοῦ Χριστοῦ, ἀλλ' οἱ ἐν πασῇ τῇ οἰκουμένῃ πιστοί, προσέθηκε τὸ, καὶ μέλη. Εἰ γὰρ καὶ σῶμα ὁλόκληρον ἦσαν, ἀλλ' οὖν μέλη· καὶ ταῦτα ἐκ μέρους, τουτέστι πάντα τὰ μέλη, ἀλλ' ἐκ μέρους. Κατὰ μὲν γὰρ τὴν ἐν ὑμῖν ἐκκλησίαν, σῶμα Χριστοῦ ἐστε, ὡς ὁλόκληρος ἐκκλησία· πρὸς δὲ τὴν ἀπανταχοῦ τῆς οἰκουμένης καθολικὴν ἐκκλησίαν, ἧς τὸ σῶμα συνέστηκεν ἐκ τῶν ἀπανταχοῦ ἐκκλησιῶν, ἔχον κεφαλὴν τὸν Χριστὸν, μέλη ἐστὶ, ἐκ τοῦ εἶναι μέρος πρὸς αὐτήν.—THEOPHYLACT. *in* 1 Cor. xii. 27, tom. ii. p. 200.

Ὅτι γὰρ τὸ ἄθροισμα τῶν ἁγίων τὸ ἐξ ὀρθῆς πίστεως καὶ πολιτείας ἀρίστης συγκεκροτημένον ἐκκλησία ἐστὶ, δῆλόν ἐστι τοῖς σοφίας γευσαμένοις.—ISODOR. *Pelus.* lib. ii. lit. 246, p. 286.

" Rudem tibi apertamque animi mei sententiam proferam, in illâ esse Ecclesiâ permanendum, quæ ab apostolis fundata usque ad diem hanc durat."—HIERON. *D. adv. Lucifer*, c. xxii. tom. ii. 201.

SERMON II.

PART I.

THE CHURCH.

Acts ii. 4.

" And the Lord added to the Church daily such as
should be saved."

" THE Faith of a Christian, as the state
of Christ's Church now stands, and shall
continue to the end of the world, consists in this, that it is an assent unto
truths credible upon the testimony of
God delivered unto us in the writings of
the Apostles and Prophets." Of these Pearson on
writings, which need no unwritten Tra- the Creed,
Art. I.
dition to bolster them up, as though
maimed and imperfect and unable to
stand alone, we have already spoken,
and the sum of what was spoken is this,

"Holy Scripture containeth all things necessary to salvation; so that whatsoever is not read therein, nor may be proved thereby, is not to be required of any man, that it should be believed as an Article of the Faith, or be thought **Art. VII.** requisite or necessary to salvation."

Next in order, Christian Brethren, we are to speak of that body, of which Christ, as Head of all things, is in an especial manner the Head; inasmuch as God, who is over all, "*Hath put all things under His feet, and gave Him to be the Head over all things to the* CHURCH, WHICH IS HIS BODY, *the fulness of Him* **Ephes. i.** *that filleth all in all.*" In other words, **22, 23.** we are to speak for the present of Holy Church—the Holy Catholic Church— one Catholic and Apostolic Church— which, in our Creeds, we profess to believe in—that "Holy Church throughout all the world" that doth acknowledge "the Father of an infinite Majesty," His "honourable, true, and only Son; also, the Holy Ghost, the Com- **Te Deum,** forter;" for such, shortly summed up, is **&c.**

the Church of those who profess and call themselves Christians.

And it is to be noted at starting that the very name of "CHURCH" doth refer us to our Lord and Saviour, for it meaneth THE HOUSE OF the LORD; that is to say, of the Lord Christ: (Οἶκος Κυριακός· *Kyriac, Kyrk,* and *Church,*) for which the Apostles (and Greek and Latin writers after them) use the term "*Ecclesia* [1]," signifying "*a calling forth,* if we look upon the origination; a congregation of men, or a company assembled, if we consider the use of it." More fully expressed, "The Church is the multitude and number of those whom Almighty God severeth from the rest of the world by the work of His grace, and

Pearson, *ut suprà.*

---

[1] All that is wanting on this head may be seen in Bp. Pearson's Notes to his Exposition of the Creed, Art. IX., and in Book i. c. 5, of "Field Of the Church." See also Beveridge on Art. XIX., Notes; and Jer. Taylor, x. 332; Jackson's Works, vol. iii. 811, folio. Two easily accessible works may here also be referred to,—Abp. Potter on Church Government, and Rogers on the Visible and Invisible Church. They contain general information on many points referred to in this sermon.

calleth to the participation of eternal happiness, by the knowledge of such supernatural verities as concerning their everlasting good He hath revealed in Christ his Son, and such other precious and happy means as He hath appointed to further and set forward the work of their salvation. So that it is the work of grace, and the heavenly calling, that give being to the Church, and make it a different society from all other companies of men in the world, that have no other light of knowledge, nor motion of desire, but that which is natural; whence, for distinction from them, it is named Field of the Church, i. 6. '*Ecclesia*,' a multitude called out." And thus, referring the word Church to Christ, as its Head, we distinguish it from the Synagogue, or Jewish Church, and restrict it to "that mystical body" of God's eternal and everlasting "Son, which is the blessed company of all faith- Com. Serv. ful people." Wide, then, and broad, and comprehensive is the term, Christian Brethren, and many there be, of God's great mercy, within its bounds; many

more than we know of, or can conceive,
—ay, " *ten thousand times ten thousand,
and thousands of thousands !* "   Rev. v. 11.

And thus, without descending to mi-
nuter particulars, we do readily conclude
that the Church we are here speaking of
is not any bare fabric of morter and
stone, such as the one we are now assembled in, but something quick, and alive,
and privileged to taste that " *the Lord is
gracious.*" And the words of St. Peter
are very applicable, inasmuch as they do
down at once with that vulgar error,
which would restrict the word Church
to the clergy alone, who, in truth, are
but a small part of it,—" *Your servants
for Jesus' sake.*" And what is it that 2 Cor. iv. 5.
St. Peter says, summoning all to that
" *living stone, disallowed indeed of men,
but chosen of God, and precious !*" Even
this : " YE ALSO, *as lively stones, are built
up a spiritual house, an holy priesthood,
to offer up spiritual sacrifices, acceptable
to God by Jesus Christ.*" Thus is the 1 Pet. ii.
4, 5.
Church dispersed throughout the whole
world; and hence (with a possible allu-

sion to Jewish restriction) called
Catholic [2], or Universal; a thing of life;
a body, that setteth not up itself above
Christ [3], but alive only *by* and *through*
Christ, which is its life-giving Head.

But, if we would arrive at the true
nature of the Church, of which we all
here are members, we must "*search the
Scriptures*," which speak of it; from
which Scriptures also we conclude that
"the visible Church of Christ" (so called,
it is likely, with reference to the *invisible*,
which contains *all Christians*—the living,
and all who have departed this life in
the Faith of Christ [4]), "is a congrega-

[2] This is very plainly put by Bp. Bull in his "Corruptions of the Church of Rome," § 1. "By the
Catholic Church, I mean the Church Universal, &c."
vol. ii. 242.—BARTON.

[3] The words alluded to are Augustine's—" Non
debet se ecclesia Christo præponere," &c. Contra
Crescon. Grammaticum, lib. ii. c. 21, tom. ix. 422.
"And therefore," says Jewel, who applies them, "we
appeal from the Church to Christ," &c. Vol. iii. 213.
Ed. Jelf.

[4] Dr. Hey adds, "Perhaps the term '*visible*' might
be used in order to prevent the Romanists from ob-
jecting; and to satisfy the *Calvinists* that it was not
intended to speak here of the *elect* or *predestinate*, as

tion of faithful men, in the which the pure Word of God is preached, and the Sacraments be duly ministered according to Christ's ordinance in all those things that of necessity are required to the same [5]." These, and such as these, are a holy temple unto the Lord. They be " the good and faithful, and the holy servants of God, scattered every where, and combined by a spiritual union in the same communion of Sacraments, whether they know one another by face or no."

Art. XIX.

Jer. Tayl. Dissuasive, &c. vol. x. p. 335.

To turn then to the Bible, and therein to "*the testimony of Jesus*," which is "*the Spirit of Prophecy*," for other prophetical prediction need we none. Whereupon observe, when our blessed Lord said unto Peter, "*I say also unto thee, That thou art Peter, and upon this rock I will build my Church; and the*

Rev. xix. 10. See Field, book ii. c. 49.

seen by God Himself." Book IV. Art. xix. § 9. The Romanists speak of " pretended invisible Church of the Heretikes," on Acts ii. 47. Rhemish Testament.

[5] See also the Second Part of the Homily for Whitsuntide, *ad init.*

gates of hell shall not prevail against it [6]*,"* He spoke of what at that time was not, but was to be. And the time drew nigh. And after He had called His Apostles, and instructed them, and other seventy also, in the mysteries of the kingdom of heaven, He completed the great work of our salvation, which He was manifest in the flesh to accomplish, and by His death did purchase unto Himself an universal Church—the household of God bought with the price of His own most precious blood. And then, after He had arisen from the dead for our justification, He arranged with the Apostles He had chosen (not, observe, with Peter alone, but equally with all) for its perpetual government. *"All power is given unto me in heaven and in earth,"* were His all sacred words. *"Go ye therefore, and teach all nations,"* (*Marg.* make disciples or Christians of all nations;) *"baptizing them in the name of the Father, and of*

---

[6] This text is not particularly dwelt upon here, but, uncontroversially, in the next Discourse.

the Son, and of the Holy Ghost. Teach-
ing them to observe all things, whatsoever
I have commanded you ; and, lo, I am
with you alway, even unto the end of the
world.——Amen." Thus, *" through the Holy* Matt.
Ghost " spake He *"unto the Apostles* xxviii.
18—20.
whom he had chosen : To whom also He
showed himself alive after His passion by
many infallible proofs, being seen of them
forty days, and speaking of the things per-
taining to the kingdom of God." After Acts i. 2, 3.
which, within ten days, the Holy Ghost
came down upon them, and their commission was complete, and they spake
" with other tongues," and began to gather Acts ii. 4.
into Christ's Church those called out
from the rest of the world.

Certainly, next to that *" upper room,"* Acts i. 13.
and other like societies, if such there
were—and after the day of Pentecost
was come and gone——then do we see the
Church going forth, in the power of the
Lord Christ, conquering and to conquer ;
and those prophetic words of Isaiah were
no dead letter, but a vital and a living
truth : *" It shall come to pass in the last*

days, that the mountain of the Lord's house," (that is to say, the Christian Church,) *" shall be established on the top of the mountains, and shall be exalted above the hills ; and all nations shall flow unto it. And many people shall go and say, Come ye, and let us go up to the mountain of the Lord, to the house of the God of Jacob ; and He will teach us of His ways, and we will walk in His paths : for out of Zion shall go forth the law, and the word of the Lord from Jerusalem [7]."* Thence went forth the perfect law of

See Vitringa in v. 2, & c. 6. Ps. ii. 6.

Isa. ii. 2, 3.

[7] Jerome's comment on these words is, "Sed et in Jerusalem primum fundata Ecclesia TOTIUS ORBIS ECCLESIAS seminavit," in loc. tom. iv. p. 33; and to the same purpose are the words in the Epist. Synod. Con. Constan. in Theodoret: Τῆς δέ γε μητρὸς ἀπασῶν τῶν ἐκκλησιῶν τῆς ἐν Ἱεροσολύμοις· lib. v. c. ix. tom. iii. 717. D. So that Bp. Bull's words are altogether to the purpose, "Doubtless this prerogative of honour was originally due to the mother or original Church. Such the Church of Rome was not, but one of the younger daughters of Sion. The Christian Church, planted at Jerusalem, was really and truly the seminary of all Christianity over the whole world."— *Vindication,* &c., vol. ii. 199. It should be added, that in point of time, Tertullian's testimony precedes all here quoted. See De Præscriptione Hær. c. xx. Routh, Scrip. Eccl. Opuscula, i. 133.

liberty—thence, very quickly, ran the word. For, scarcely can it be necessary to remind you of its free course, and how what his Lord prophesied of Peter was presently fulfilled. Not a tittle of it fell to the ground. Yea, rather, when Peter had, by his prolific sermon, converted " *three thousand souls,*" which were added unto the " *hundred and twenty* " disciples, then was there a Church, (and that built upon Peter, according to our Lord's promise,) for after that we read, as it is in the words of the text : " *The Lord added to the Church daily such as should be saved.*"

Acts ii. 41. i. 15.

But and if, as we learn from those Scriptures, which, unto us, are the only sure record of God's truth, the Church of Christ is declared to have gone forth from Jerusalem, strange and presumptuous, no less than false, palpably false, is that Romanist assertion, that Rome is the *mother* and the *mistress* of all other Churches ; yea, more than assertion—a profession also, to which (on oath) "all beneficed clergymen belonging to the

E

Church of Rome are bound to subscribe, not only by the Bull of Pius IV., but by a decree of the Council of Trent [8]," the words of which are quoted in the Bull itself, and run thus: "I acknowledge the Holy Catholic and Apostolic Church of Rome to be the mother and mistress of all Churches." Whereto it is added: "I promise to swear true obedience to the Roman Pontiff, successor of the Prince of the Apostles, St. Peter, and the Vicegerent (or Vicar) of Jesus Christ;" — an unhallowed assumption never acknowledged by the Catholic Church, which the Church of Rome is not, notwithstanding her never-ceasing and intrusive claim!

Passing, however, this assumption by, it is more to our present purpose to remark, that after the word of the Lord was gone forth from Jerusalem, the con-

---

[8] See Bp. Marsh's Comparative View, c. vi. pp. 121. 125, 2nd edition; and Bp. Beveridge's Sermon 2 Tim. i. 13, vol. ii. 202. Ed. Horne. Certainly we might ask with St. Paul, "*What! came the word of God out from you? or came it to you only?*"—1 Cor. xiv. 36.

verts, any where, were called the Church;
not the whole Church, but, after Apostolic order and constitution, the Church
of that place, city, nation, province, kingdom. And thus, connected with the
body, and with Christ, the Head, were
there many Churches, so to say, scattered abroad. *Many* in one sense, *one*
in another. For, as you, and I, and
every private Christian, is a member of
some particular Church, so is every particular Church a member of the Catholic
or Universal, which is always meant
when we read in Scripture of the Church
in general, without the addition of place
or country. As where it is said, that
" *Christ also loved the Church,*" and
" *Christ is the Head of the Church ;*" and Ephes. v.
in the text, " *The Lord added to the* 25, 23.
Church daily such as should be saved ;" Beveridge,
or, if you like, such as are saved [9]—called ii. 143.

---

[9] The original, as is well known, is τοὺς σωζομένους ;
the common version would require σωθησομένους. But,
whichever way rendered, it is of little matter, and
any Calvinistic pressure is unavailing. See the remarks of Jackson : " Some there be who define this
Church to be *cœtus prædestinatorum,*" &c. vol. iii. 816.

out from the world that lieth in wickedness, and put into the way of salvation, after His teaching who is "*the way, the truth, and the life.*"

John xiv. 6.

And here, if it be asked what this way was, the same Scriptures are not slow to inform us. It was after the same way the three thousand were added on the day of Pentecost, of whom it is written, "*they that gladly received his word* WERE BAPTIZED;" therein following the institution of our Lord and Saviour, who had said, "*He that believeth and is baptized shall be saved.*" Such was the door of entrance into the Christian Church; and of those who so entered the same Scripture saith, "*they continued stedfastly in the Apostles' doctrine and fellowship, and in the breaking of bread, and in prayers.*" In other words. They held close "to the communion and fellowship of the Apostles, and the rest of the disciples of Christ; and constantly professed that doctrine which the Apostles taught them, and joined together in the celebration and receipt of the blessed

Acts ii. 41.

Mark xvi. 16.

Acts ii. 42.

Sacrament of the body and blood of Christ, and in prayers." Such was the Bp. Hall's Par. Hard Texts. way of them—such the early Church; furnished, within a little while, and by Apostolic direction, with her bishops, priests, and deacons, as " is evident unto all men diligently reading the Holy Scriptures and ancient authors." And Pref. to Ord. Services. that in His own appointed way, the Lord would have His people added to His Church, He gave a striking instance for evermore in the cases of Cornelius the good centurion, Candace's eunuch, and in Paul the Apostle, whom Ananias baptized for this very thing. And hence, See Acts ix. 18. from Christ's own command, that constant expression of the early days of Christianity, " Without the Church there is no salvation [10];" that is to say, no revealed mode of salvation.

And the sum of what has been said is

---

[10] St. Cyprian, Epist. iv. § 4.—" Neque enim vivere foris possunt ; cum domus Dei una sit, et *nemini salus esse nisi in Ecclesia possit*." It is, in fact (not to mention Augustine and others), the constant teaching of St. Cyprian. See particularly Epist. lxxiv. *Pompeio Fratri.*

this: There is one Catholic or Universal Church, redeemed by the precious blood of Christ, *"out of every kindred, and* Rev. v. 10. *tongue, and people, and nation* [11]*;"* one, nevertheless, because, according to the Almighty's purpose, many members are knit together into one body, by one Spirit, under one Head, which is Christ. Even as the Apostle saith, *" There is one body, and one Spirit, even as ye are called in one hope of your calling: one Lord, one faith, one Baptism, one God and Father of all, who is above all, and through all, and in you all.   But unto every one of us is given grace according* Ephes. iv. *to the measure of the gift of Christ."* Such 4—7. is the Church inwardly and essentially. Outwardly, however, it is even as we

[11] Jackson refers to this text as one where "the full importance of this term Catholic is set down." See vol. iii. 821.   He had before beautifully observed, " Though we be washed with the water of Baptism, and with the wine of the Eucharist in this life, yet cannot we be so washed or cleansed as to be left without spot, wrinkle, or blemish, until we have put off this earthly tabernacle, either by death, or by that change whereunto all are subject that shall not die."—Ibid. p. 820. Book xii. c. 4.

see and know it to be,—that is to say, a visible society of many churches, national, congregational, or other, with names "betokening severalty, as the Church of Rome, Corinth, Ephesus, England, and so the rest," even to the congregational Church in which we are now assembled, and other the many churches of our land, which, with other churches militant in all lands, are part and parcel of that one Catholic and Universal Church, of which Christ alone is Head. Holy, moreover, is the Church, notwithstanding the wrinkles, and spots, and blemishes of mortality; for unto it the holiness of its Head, which is Christ, is imputed, "*who loved the Church, and gave Himself for it; that He might sanctify and cleanse it with the washing of water by the word, that He might present it unto Himself a glorious Church, not having spot or wrinkle, or any such thing; but that it should be holy and without blemish.*"

Such, Christian Brethren, is the Holy Catholic Church in which we believe,

Hooker, Ecc. Pol. iii. ii. § 1.

Ephes. v. 25—27.

Art. XXI.

Pacian. in
Epist. i. ad
Sempron. [12]
apud Field
of the
Church,
book ii.
c. ix. folio.

Jude, 3.

"a witness and a keeper of Holy Writ." Neither do we claim to ourselves, exclusive of others, the name of Catholic. The rather, in the words of an old worthy, we do say individually, "Christian is my name, and Catholic is my surname; by the one I am known from Infidels; by the other from Heretics and Schismatics."

And this brings me to the painful part of the subject in hand. I say painful, because discussion is ever so in this Holy Place, and unbefitting those whose "*sin is ever before*" them, and never to be justified but when "*we should earnestly contend for the faith which was once delivered to the saints.*" Therefore do I speak to you of the "*common salvation,*" because, unto us the Romanists deny it to be "*common.*" Not to disguise plain words, they call us HERETICS, without the pale and without the protection of Holy Church. Give ear, then,

[12] The passage alluded to by Field is in Epist. i. § 7, " Of the Catholic Name ;" and is rather the substance than a literal translation.

whilst I speak very shortly and very plainly on this head.

I. The Church of Rome declareth that she alone is the Catholic Church, without whose bounds there is no salvation; calling herself, withal, the mistress and the mother of all churches. And to these points it has been answered in what has been already said. For, unless a part (as we believe, a sickly and an unhealthy part) can be taken for the whole [13], Catholic, in her own sense, she is not. Mistress also and mother of all churches she cannot be, as God's Word is true; for the word of the Lord went forth from Jerusalem; there the Church began, and there it received addition and increase.

II. But all of this they deny, though it

---

[13] Bp. Bull's words are, "To say either of the Church of Rome, or of the Church of England, or of the Greek Church, or of any other particular Church, of what denomination soever, that it is the Catholic or Universal Church, would be as absurd as to affirm that a part is the whole."—*Corruptions of the Church of Rome*, § 2, vol. ii. 244. See also Scott's Christian Life, Works, vol. ii. 498.

stands in the forefront of God's Holy Book. St. Peter, they say, is the Head of the Church, the bishops of Rome his successors; not a word of which appears in the Bible. Bishop of •Rome it cannot be proved that he ever was: those also there are who doubt whether he ever was at Rome or not [14]. But, to let that pass, and to speak of the Supremacy which they ground on such words of Scripture as "*Upon this Rock will I build my Church.*" "*Feed my sheep.*" Comforting and encouraging words, certainly, to one so earnest as Peter; to one who had so fallen as to deny his Lord and Master! Yet doth the rest of Scripture give no countenance to the interpretation of them after the fashion

Matt. xvi. 18. John xxi. 15—17.

[14] Bp. Pearson, in his " Dissertatio Prima de Serie et Successione Primorum Romæ Episcorum," c. vii., maintains that he was there. See Minor Theol. Works, vol. ii. 329, &c. That he was at all concerned in the foundation of the Church of Rome cannot easily be maintained ; as Bp. Marsh says, " We must either renounce the opinion, or let Scripture give way to tradition." See *Comparative View,* c. x. p. 208. But, see Bp. Bull's Vindication of the Church of England, § xix. vol. ii. 196, &c.

of Rome. What was granted to Peter was repeated to the rest of the Apostles; and then, for feeding the flock, and gently leading the sheep of the Christian fold, St. Paul "*was not a whit behind the very chiefest Apostles.*" Then, as regards 2 Cor. xi. 5. xii. 11. the Apostles themselves, they clearly never so understood our Saviour's words as giving to Peter either precedency or authority; for to the very last, "THEY DISPUTED AMONG THEMSELVES WHO SHOULD BE THE GREATEST:" words Mark ix. 33. which, to a plain, simple, unbiassed understanding, should be decisive on the subject [15].

The real truth of the matter is, that originally the pre-eminence of one Church over another was but "an institution of men for convenience and order," and great cities [16] had precedence See Secker, vi. 404.

[15] The reader is referred to Overall's Convocation Book, book ii. c. xi., " That there is no more necessity of one visible head of the Church, than of one visible monarch of the world."

[16] As regards Rome, the sixth canon of the Council of Nice, A.D. 325, shows clearly that no precedence, as the Romanists understand precedence, was granted

only according to their name. Such was
Rome, the then mistress of the world;
and the precedence once granted to her
in Ecclesiasticals was afterwards claimed
as a right, and by wicked hands and cunning sleights, as far as might be, retained and kept. Denied, however, was
it on all sides, as history recounts; and
the claim to precedency and Supremacy, which drew in its train the title
of Universal Bishop, was scouted out as
preposterous. Insomuch so, that "in the
sixth century, when the Emperor Mau-
ritius continued a practice begun by
some prior emperor, to give the Bishop
of Constantinople" (or, New Rome,) "the
title of Universal Bishop, Pelage, and
after him Gregory the Great, broke out
into the most pathetical expressions that
could be invented against it; he compared it to the pride of Lucifer; and

to her, but that her jurisdiction was limited like that
of other churches and patriarchs. Τὰ ἀρχαῖα ἔθη
κρατείτω κ.τ.ἐ. See *Routh, Script. Eccles. Opusc.*
i. 358. For full information, the Ninth Book of Bingham should be referred to.—Palmer's Treatise on the
Church, vol. ii. 478, &c. Part vii.

said that *he who assumed it was the fore-runner of Antichrist* [17]; and as he re-nounced all claim to it, so he affirmed, that none of his predecessors had ever aspired to such a power." So little is there in Scripture or in history to bolster up the unhallowed assumption. And it is as one said, " If, in a foresight of this usurpation, Gregory should have been hired to have spoken for us against the pride of his following successors, he could not have set a keener edge upon his style."

Burnet on Art. XXXVII.

Bp. HALL, " The Old Religion," c. xvii.

III. But if this boasted claim of Supremacy falls to the ground, even as it does, so with it must the claim to Infallibility, likewise ; and, certainly, when we look

[17] Almost all writers refer to these words of Gregory. See Jewel's Works, vol. ii. 143. 203, and vii. 174, on 2 Thess. ii. 7. " What said a Pope of their own, even Gregory ? ' Fidenter dico, quod quisquis se universalem Sacerdotem vocat, vel vocari desiderat, in elatione suâ Antichristum præcurrit,' " lib. vi. Epist. 30, vol. ii. 881. See likewise the *Apologia*, p. 23. Dr. Jelf's New Edit. for the Soc. for Prom. Christian Knowledge ; Field of the Church, book v. c. 32, p. 518 ; and Mixed Authorities on Perkins' Reformed Catholike, vol. i. 609.

into the New Testament for any visible Head of the Church we find it not; when we search there for Infallibility we find it not. The promise of perpetuity we do find; for Christ, as the Head, will never fail His Church; yea, "though the providence of God doth suffer many particular churches to cease, yet the promise of the same God will never permit that all of them at once shall perish." Whereupon, finding in the Scriptures neither Supremacy nor Infallibility attached to the Church of Rome, we do deny her claim to be the Catholic Church, conceding her nevertheless to be a Particular Church, which she doth not concede to us. Nay, more; we assert that "as the Church of Jerusalem, Alexandria, and Antioch have erred, so also the Church of Rome hath erred, not only in their living and manner of ceremonies, but also in matters of faith."

Hence, at the Reformation, we separated from her errors—not from the Holy Catholic Church; for "we hope that to reform ourselves, if at any time

Pearson on the Creed, Art. IX.

Art. XX.

we have done amiss, is not to sever ourselves from the Church we were of before. In the Church we were, and we Hooker,
are so still." Our Church—as a part of iii. 1. 10.
the Catholic or Universal Church—is
just where it was before the days of
Luther [18], only purified, cleansed, swept,
garnished. It is to be found, where the
Church of Rome as now constituted cannot be found—in the Holy Scriptures,
in the writings of the ancient Fathers,
in the records of Councils, in the testimony of all the early ages, or ever error
was set up in the place of truth, and
Decretals were forged, and a Boniface
(VIII.) had the boldness to say, "it was
necessary for every man to be subject
to the Pope's authority." And the answer of Dinothus, the learned abbot of
Bangor, when Augustine, as Pope Gregory's legate, required submission from

---

[18] The old Romanist question, " Where was your
Church before Luther ?" See Perkins, vol. i. 310.
610 ; Hooker's Eccles. Pol. iii. 1. 10 ; " Field, of the
Church," book iii. c. viii. p. 84 ; Abp. Sharpe, vol. v.
329 ; Secker, vi. 406 ; Bp. Hall, vol. i. 633, &c. &c.

the British Church to the Bishop of Rome is never to be forgotten; for he replied in the name of all the Britons, "That they knew no obedience due to him whom they called the Pope, but the obedience of love; and that, under God, they were governed by the Bishop of Caerleon;" that is to say, a primate and patriarchal bishop of their own land [19].

See Bp. Bull's "Corruptions of the Church of Rome," vol. ii. 291.

But, although we make these references to days gone by—to history, to fathers, or to councils—yet they are not our stronghold. No! here, as elsewhere, we "*search the Scriptures*" to find out what the Church is, and who they are that are rightly grafted into it. And

[19] The authenticity of this reply, as is well known, has been disputed; but the substance of it is given in these other words of Bede, " At illi nil horum se facturos, neque illum pro archiepiscopo habituros," &c. lib. ii. 2. See the original reply in Latin and Welsh, apud Smith, Appendix, No. x. p. 716, and the remarks of Collier, Book ii. Cent. vii. vol. i. p. 76. Lappenberg argues for the authenticity of the reply. The reader may see the more modern orthography of Dinooth's reply in the Clar. edit. of Fuller, vol. i. 150, note n n. Speaking of Bede's Eccl. Hist. I must by all means mention Professor Hussey's excellent edition of it.

this search has been laid before you. No reason is it that we should "give over the right and inheritance we have in the Church of God, for that" Romanists, "by intrusion and unjust means, have entituled" themselves "unto the same. It behoveth us rather to search the Scriptures, as Christ hath advised us, and thereby to assure ourselves of the Church of God. For by this trial only, and by none other, it may be known." Other false trials we leave to those, who, though they admit the Scriptures to be infallibly true, do not admit them (as before shown) to be an infallible rule, and therefore seek elsewhere with their adventitious Tradition, proclaiming the Church, and not the Scriptures "to be the infallible judge and measure of our Faith," which is to give us our Rule. We "blear not the eyes of the simple sort with such their vain illusions;" we bid them read for themselves, and follow after "the pattern and sampler of Christ and his Apostles' in-

See JEWEL Defence of Apol. vol. iv. 144.

Jer. Tayl. x. 332.

Overall's Conv. book ii. xi.

F

Jewel, Ibid.
iv. 338. stitution." For those who are unlearned and cannot read,—the instructions proposed for coming at the knowledge of Scripture are equally applicable here.

One other remark only need be made on the pretensions of the Romish Church to Infallibility, which is this: that if it fail in one point, it fails in all. That it doth so fail, the contradictions amongst themselves are a standing proof. I instance, in passing, that the Council of Constance, in opposition to the subsequent Councils of Florence and the fifth Lateran, defined a Council to be above the Pope[20]. Neither need be right; but one decision must gainsay the other, and, as in other cases, deal hardly with their pretended Infallibility. Generally, I believe, the teaching of Rome is, that

---

[20] Jeremy Taylor adds, " The Council of Basil, all the world knows how greatly they asserted their own authority over the Pope; but therefore, though in France it is accepted, yet in Italy and Spain it is not." Of the Church, Dissuasive, vol. x. p.. 368. See Jewel's words, in Epist. de Concil. Tridentino, vol. viii. 90.

a General Council confirmed by the Pope is to be relied upon as "the supreme judge and determiner of questions." Against such a conclusion, referring to Holy Scripture only for decided proof, we protest in our twenty-first Article. But, Christian Brethren, all this jarring of discussion is but as the jostling and shouldering of wave against wave, in " *a place where two seas meet ;*" and therefore, with an apology almost, I pass it by, as irrelevant to a Manual so plain as this is intended to be,—simply adding, that the Church of Rome teaches " that we are to judge of doctrines by the authority and decisions of the Church; whereas we affirm, that we are first to examine the doctrine, and according to that to judge of the purity of the Church." Willingly indeed do we hear the voice of Holy Mother Church, when she speaketh " *as the oracles of God,*" even as speak she doth alway! But and if any particular Church speak otherwise (as, for instance, the Church of Rome),

Jer. Tayl. x. 358.

Acts xxvii. 41.

Burnet on Art. XIX.

1 Pet. iv. 11.

F 2

then we do hear God rather, seeking forthwith "*to the law and to the testimony*." And when we admit, as we do, that the Church to which we are privileged to belong "hath power to decree rites or ceremonies, and authority in

Art. XX. controversies of Faith," we admit it upon no infallible claim, but in accordance only with Scripture, and consistently with that system of religious liberty with which Christ hath made us free, and with a judgment unfettered from that religious slavery which binds down to contradictions the members of the Church of Rome. And thus under-

FIELD, Of the Church, book iv. c. 8. p. 358 stood, " it is true that the authority of God's Church prepareth us unto the Faith, and serveth as an introduction to bring us to the discerning, and perfect apprehension of Divine things, but is not the ground of our Faith and reason of believing. And that, doubtless, is the meaning of the words of St. Augustine," who so often elsewhere speaks of the supremacy of Scripture, "that he would not believe the Gospel if the authority of the Church did not move him thereto[21]."

And thus do we, whom the Romanists call Heretics, believe, not in their particular, but in the Holy Catholic Church; and each plain Christian man may make answer for himself in those words of Paul to Felix, saying, "*Neither can they prove the things whereof they now accuse me. But this I confess unto thee, that after the way which they call heresy, so worship I the God of my fathers, believing all things which are written in the law and in the prophets.*"

Acts xxiv. 13, 14.

Two points yet remain, which must be touched upon shortly. The first is, how can Rome, with errors such as she maintains, and which will be laid before you hereafter in detail, be called a Church at all? The answer to which is, that,

---

[21] " St. Augustine, ye say, holdeth hard of your side. He saith, ' *Non crederem evangelio, nisi me ecclesiæ catholicæ auctoritas commoveret,*'" &c. Contra Epist. Fundam. c. 5, tom. viii. 154. The reader should refer to the whole of the Extracts on Jewel, Defence of the Apology, vol. vi. 149, 150.

notwithstanding her errors, she holds to
the foundation,—to the fundamentals of
the Christian Faith,—though foisting in
together with "*wood, hay, stubble*," the
" *stones of emptiness*," likewise.   In the
words of judicious Hooker, "Many things
exclude from the kingdom of God,
although from the Church they separate
not.   Both heresy and *many other crimes*,
which *wholly sever from God*, do sever
from the Church of God *in part only*,"
as instanced in the idolatrous Jews in
the Old Testament, who, for all their
idolatry, were borne up with still.   "That
which separateth *utterly*, that which
cutteth off *clean* from the visible Church
of Christ, is plain Apostasy, *direct* denial,
utter rejection of the whole Christian
Faith as far as the same is professedly
different from infidelity."   This certainly
is not the case with the Romanists ; for
however much they have swerved aside
like a broken bow, they do hold to Christ
the Head ; and even if "the very true
Church of Christ they have left, howbeit " they have " not altogether left nor

1 Cor. iii.
12.
Isa. xxxiv.
11.

forsaken simply the Church, upon the main foundations whereof they continue built, notwithstanding these breaches whereby they are *rent at the top* asunder." Hooker, Eccl. Pol. book v. lxviii. 6, 7. As another great divine expresses it, "We are all the same Church, by the virtue of our outward vocation, whosoever, all the world over, worship Jesus Christ, the only Son of God, and Saviour of the world, and profess the same common Creed. Some of us do this more purely; others more corruptly. In the mean time, we are all Christians, but sound Christians we are not. That which Rome holds with us, makes it a Church; that which it obtrudes upon us, makes it heretical. The truth of principle makes it one; the error and impiety of additions make it irreconcileable." And Bp. Hall, "No Peace with Rome," §1. thus, admitting Rome to be a true Church, we cannot communicate with her, as long as she teaches the unscriptural doctrines she doth. Her Traditions, and maiming of the Sacrament of the Lord's Supper—to say nothing of her impositions and enchantments—we cannot away with. They are snares for simple souls. And therefore do we say, "*Come out from among them, and be ye separate, and touch not the unclean thing.*"

2 Cor. vi. 7.

The other point not to be passed over is this:—If we, in separating from the corruptions of the Romish Church, were not guilty of schism [22] in the Romish sense, which always includes *sinful* division—can those who separate from us, following in our particular Church the teaching and order of the Apostles, with a properly ordained Ministry, and a regular Episcopate — can they, the

[22] I do not know any accessible writer who has treated this delicate point more clearly than Bp. Marsh, in his Comparative View. See c. viii. Note C in the Appendix has a simple explanation of the word σχίσμα. It is quite clear, on the principle of infallibility, that *schisma* and *schismaticus*, to a Romanist, must convey the notion of *sin ;* to a Protestant it need not necessarily do so, however great the evil of division, which is at once admitted. It is observable that our Reformers avoided the use of the term—that it does not occur in our Articles, nor even in the *text* of the Canons. In the two places in our Liturgy where the word occurs—in the Service for the King's Accession, and in the Litany—it did not proceed from the Reformers, but was an after addition.

mingled Dissenters of modern days, be clear on their secession in the sight of God? Whereupon arises another form of the question: If they secede from a Church which has grown up after the following of the Apostles, are they of the Church? As regards the latter portion of the question, there can be no hesitation in making answer, THEY ARE; for although "there is not the least contention and variance, but it blemisheth somewhat the unity that ought to be in the Church of Christ," yet "as long as both parts retain by outward profession that vital substance of truth which maketh Christian religion to differ from those which acknowledge not our Lord Jesus Christ the blessed Saviour of mankind, give no credit to His glorious Gospel, and have His Sacraments, the seals of eternal life, in derision;"—as long as this is not denied, it cannot be said with truth that seceders are not of the Church.— As regards the former part of this question, there likewise can be no doubt also but that any one who, without a

Hooker, Eccl. Pol. lxviii. 6.

just cause, separateth himself from a Church, in which "the pure word of God is preached, and the Sacraments be duly ministered according to Christ's ordinance in all those things that of necessity are requisite to the same," is *guilty of sin.* If he be unruly, self-willed, envious, ambitious, like Diotrephes

3 John 9. loving to have "*the pre-eminence*," and so depart, because the Church in which he is brought up admitteth none such evil customs—*he is guilty of sin.* If he be heady and high-minded in the midst of ignorance, declining to be taught the truth of God, as taught in the Church wherein he was born and baptized, and so depart—*he too is guilty of sin.* And I do not hesitate to say, that for the most part Dissent has arisen from these causes. "*These be they who separate*

Jude 19. *themselves, sensual, not having the Spirit.*" Other causes there are, such as neglect of duties on our own parts; and for these (which I do not dwell upon particularly) we must pray God to pardon us, and to add yet *daily to His Church such as shall be saved.* But and if none of these intervene, and one, conscientiously and devoutly, cannot conclude the Church to which he belongs, and in which he was brought up, to be a spiritual Church, is such an one to be branded as an apostate and "*cast out,*" like the poor blind John ix. 34. man whom the Lord Jesus restored to sight? Certainly not! for by so doing we should deprive a brother of that liberty of private judgment we won back at the Reformation. This right, Bp. in fact, "is founded on the same princi- Marsh's ple as that by which the Church of Eng- View, land seceded from the Church of Rome;" note ᵉ. and however much we may deplore the division, sin in such separation there is none, or the right of conscience were null and void. And applicable here are those words of Moses, the meekest of men, when it was reported unto him that Eldad and Medad, out of due order somewhat, did "*prophesy in the camp;*" and Joshua, the son of Nun, did wish him to forbid it: "*And Moses said unto him, Enviest thou for my sake? would*"

God that all the Lord's people were pro-
phets, and that the Lord would put His
Spirit upon them!" Never must we
forget our blessed Lord's words also, on
a like occasion, when John would have
had Him to forbid one that cast out devils,
"*because he followed not us,*" for He said,
"HE THAT IS NOT AGAINST US IS ON OUR
PART!"

And thus, Christian Brethren, have I
spoke unto you of the Church in all its
full broad meaning; from the single
congregation in which we are now
assembled, upward to the Holy Catholic
Church throughout the whole world;
which is, rightly understood, and measured by the Scripture, "*the Church of*
the living God, the pillar and ground of
the Faith [23]." And, having said thus much,

Numb. xi. 29.

Mark ix. 38—40.

See 1 Tim. iii. 15.

[23] It is to be noticed, that *in essentials* the Church,
as it now is, is the same with the Church of the
Apostles.   On this well-known text, which the
Rhemists say " pincheth all Heretikes wonderfully"
(Fulke in loc.), see Jac. Gothofredi, " Prior Ex-
ercitatio de Ecclesiâ Dei," in the Critici Sacri, and
Inm. Weber's Parerga Philologica ad 1 Tim. iii. 15, in
the Thesaur. Philolog. tom. ii. 653, &c. There needed

let me now add, that when all the glories
of the Church are told, none is greater
than this, that she is glorious in holiness.
"Without holiness the privileges of the Pearson on the Creed,
Church prove the greatest disadvantages; Art. IX.
and the means of salvation neglected
tend to a punishment with aggravation.
We must acknowledge a necessity of
holiness when we confess that Christ
alone, which is Holy, can make us
happy." Or, as another worthy hath it,
"It is a disgrace to the holy Church of Perkins'
God, that men, professing themselves Re-formed
the members of it, should be unholy." Catholike, vol. i.
Therefore, be ye Catholic in your lives, p. 314.
as the Church to which ye belong is
Catholic; that is to say, whole in Christ
and wanting nothing. Be not conformed
to this world, but to Him who is your
Head, and the Church's Head; and despite the babbling of Papist troublers,

no fencing with the Romanists. As Grotius said,
"Tituli hi sunt Ecclesiæ : cui, qui eos invident,
mirum quam laborant ut hæc verba (i. e. στύλος καὶ
ἑδραίωμα) sequenti periodo connectant," &c. Add to
the above the Answer of Cranmer to Smythe's Preface, vol. iii. 19, &c. Ed. *Jenkyns*.

rest assured, that once baptized unto Christ, we are " *added to the Church;* " baptized into any one congregation after the following of the Apostles, we are made component members of that spiritual body against which " *the gates of hell* " shall avail nothing!

And I shall conclude this point in the well-known words of one who spoke boldly, as he ought to speak : " So long as you continue in our communion, you are in the communion of the true Church of Christ, and in an infinitely safer communion than if you were in theirs, who would entice you Romewards. I dare answer for the salvation of all those who, continuing in our Church, do live up to the principle of it; but I dare answer nothing for them, who, being brought up in this Church, and having so great opportunities given them of knowing the truth, do yet depart from it. I pray God they may be able to answer for themselves."

Forget not ever what it is your privilege to remember, that as a portion of

Abp.
Sharpe's
Sermons,
v. p. 113.

the visible Church, ye are co-partners with the invisible. What is to be, if ye continue grounded and settled in the Faith, is as though it were. In St. Paul's words, even now, abiding on the earth with your thoughts above it: "*Ye are come unto Mount Sion, and unto the city of the living God, the heavenly Jerusalem, and to an innumerable company of angels, to the general assembly of the Church of the First-born, which are written in heaven, and to God the Judge of all, and to the Spirits of just men made perfect, and to* JESUS THE MEDIATOR OF THE NEW COVENANT," &c.

Heb. xii. 22—24.

SERMON II.

PART II.

ST. PETER'S CONFESSION.

G

Τὸν καρτερὸν καὶ μέγαν τῶν ἀποστόλων, τὸν ἀρετῆς ἕνεκα τῶν λοιπῶν ἁπάντων προήγορον.—Eᴜsᴇʙ. *Eccles. Hist.* lib. ii. c. 14.

" He had a singular zeal for promoting our Lord's service, and propagation of the Gospel, therein outshining the rest, &c. This is the primacy which Eusebius attributeth to him when he calleth him the excellent and great apostle, who for his virtue was the prolocutor of the rest."—Bᴀʀʀᴏᴡ, *on the Pope's Supremacy,* vol. vii. 64.

"' *Thou art Peter,*' &c., viz. upon Him Whom thou hast now confessed to be the Son of God, or upon thy confession which thou hast made of Him. And howsoever the Church of Rome may force another sense upon the words, certainly this is the exposition which the primitive Church gave of them. Some of the Fathers expressly avouching Christ Himself to be the Rock here understood, others Peter's confession of Christ and faith in Him, all which come to one and the same thing ; ' therefore,' saith St. Augustine, ' Christ is the foundation in the structure of a wise architect.' "—Bᴘ. Bᴇᴠᴇʀɪᴅɢᴇ, *on Art. XXXVII.* ii. 396.

Οὐκ ἀγνοῶν τὴν τῶν ἀνθρώπων περὶ αὐτοῦ πολυώνυμον δόξαν ὁ τὰς καρδίας ἐμβατεύων Χριστός, ἤρετο τοὺς ἑαυτοῦ μαθητάς, Τίνα με λέγουσιν οἱ ἄνθρωποι εἶναι ; ἀλλὰ τὴν ἀσφαλῆ ὁμολογίαν διδάξαι πάντας βουλόμενος, ἣν ἐμπνευσθεὶς ὁ Πέτρος περὶ αὐτοῦ ὡς κρηπῖδα καὶ βάθρον ἀπέθετο, ἐφ' ᾗ τὴν ἑαυτοῦ ἐκκλησίαν ὁ Κύριος ᾠκοδόμησε.—Isᴏᴅᴏʀ. *Pelus. Epist.* lib. i. 235, p. 67. A.

" Brevis confessio, sed quæ totam salutis nostræ summam in se continet," &c.—Cᴀʟᴠɪɴ, *Harm. in loc.* Tholuck, ii. 106.

SERMON II.

PART II.

ST. PETER'S CONFESSION[1].

MATT. xvi. 15, 16.

" He saith unto them, But whom say ye that I am ?
And Simon Peter answered and said, Thou art the
Christ, the Son of the living God."

HE that was once so unhappy in his
denial of his Lord and Master, and had

[1] This plain Sermon, preached in the regular course
of the Lessons, September 15, 1850, and so previous to
our present commotion, was the result of reading Isaac
Casaubon's Exercitatio xv. § 12, &c., ad Annales Eccles.
Baronii, Barrow on the Supremacy, Laud's Conference
with Fisher, Bp. Croft's Legacy, Chrysostom, Theophylact, &c. &c.,—in fact, after I had arrived at,
I trust, a clear and satisfactory conclusion. I should
add, that though I do not adopt the interpretation of
the Lutheran and Calvinistic divines, because opposed
to the literal sense of Scripture, yet I combine it with

G 2

to weep so bitterly till the all-compassionate look of Christ dried up his tears, was elsewhere the readiest to confess Him; and that Lord, Who knew what was in his heart—its earnestness, its boldness, its zealous affectionateness, its unreserved devotion—forgave the iniquity of his sin, and sent him forth to feed His lambs, and to be one amongst many chief shepherds who were to fold His flock, to strengthen the diseased, to heal that which was sick, to bind up that which was broken, to bring again that which was driven away, to seek that which was lost. To this, so high a destination, was Peter called, and endowed with "many excellent gifts," and with so sure and sound a faith as in good time to die the death of a martyr for Him whom once he feared to confess; nay more, if ecclesiastical story speak

Ezek. xxxiv. 4. See Collect St. Peter's Day.

the words ἐπὶ ταύτῃ τῇ πέτρᾳ, much as Chrysostom and Theophylact do. For further general information, Faber's Difficulties of Romanism, and Palmer's Treatise of the Church, should be consulted, as easily accessible, and containing pro et con full and correct references.

true, with such a sense of utter humiliation and self-abasement as wiped off the
once self-confidence of his temper; for he
was crucified with his head downwards [2], Euseb.
declaring that he was "unworthy to E. H. lib.
iii. 1. κατὰ
suffer in the same posture wherein κεφαλῆς [2]
his Lord had suffered before him." Nelson in
loc.
This, however, is a point in which we
are no ways concerned. It is mentioned
only for as much as it is worth. Our
business is with the confession in the
text: "*Thou art the Christ, the Son of
the living God;*" and with that portion
of Scripture connected with it. At the
same time we must not forget, though

---

[2] Eusebius relates the fact on the authority of
Origen. Chrysostom several times alludes to it, as
does Jerome. See authorities in Lardner, Supplement, c. xviii. vi. § 6. The lines of Prudentius are
well known :—

" Prima Petrum rapuit sententia legibus Neronis
  Pendere jussum præminente ligno.
Ille tamen veritus celsæ decus æmulando mortis
  Ambire tanti gloriam magistri :
Exigit, ut pedibus mersum caput imprimant supinis,
  Quo spectet imum stipitem cerebro.
Figitur ergo manus subter, sola versus in cacumen
  Hoc mente major, quo minor figurâ," &c.—
          XII. Passio Petri et Pauli, v. 11, &c.

we purposely pass by the vamped-up stories of the Romish Church and the idle talk of Peter's supremacy, that he See 2 Ep. i. 14. still belonged to the noble army of martyrs, even as our Lord Jesus Christ showed him he should, saying, " *When* John xxi. 18, 19. *thou wast young, thou girdedst thyself, and walkedst whither thou wouldest ; but when thou shalt be old, thou shalt stretch forth thy hands, and another shall gird thee, and carry thee whither thou wouldest not. This spake He, signifying by what death he should glorify God.*"

But to turn to the passage of Scripture with which the text lies in immediate connexion. It was now the third year of the preaching of Jesus; and throughout the regions of Judæa, Samaria, and Galilee, He had declared by His mighty works the glory of His eternal Godhead, insomuch that, if unprejudiced, the Jews from their own Scriptures might have seen that He was that Great Prophet which was to come into the world, as well as that sure foundation Isaiah spake of in the word of the Lord, saying, "*Behold, I lay in Zion for a foundation, a stone, a tried stone, a precious corner-stone, a sure foundation.*" Isa. xxviii. 16. But, as many amongst ourselves are slow to understand what concerns our everlasting salvation, so were the Jews to understand the tokens of their Messiah. As a body, they were dreaming dreams [3] of His earthly victories, and of nations to be subdued by the power of His might. Jesus, meek and lowly, was not in all their thoughts, but a King to ride in triumph, and to deliver them from the hard yoke and thrall of Roman domination. Otherwise than His was the doctrine of the Pharisees and Sadducees; and the people were more likely

---

[3] See Lightfoot in loc. "Hebrew and Talmudical Exercit.," Works, vol. ii. 204, folio. " He asketh not," saith Theophylact, " what say the Pharisees, but, ' What say the people of me ?'—the unlettered multitude—περὶ τοῦ ἀδόλου πλήθους λέγων." Cf. in loc. tom. i. p. 84. C.

On the words " Son of Man," never applied unto our Lord but by Himself, till Stephen so applied them (Acts vii. 56), see Calvin in loc., " Nunc, dum carne indutus," &c. Harm. ii. 105. Isod. Pelusiot. has similar remarks. See Epist. iv. 236, p. 67, folio.

than *they* were to apprehend His coming.
At the least, bitter hatred and prejudice
were not so deeply seated in their nature.
And thus it chanced, "*when Jesus came
into the coasts of Cæsarea Philippi*," that
the people's notion was rather appealed
to than theirs'.   For, on that occasion,
Jesus "*asked His disciples, saying, Whom
do men say that I the Son of Man am?*"
that I, whom the prophet Daniel spake

Dan. vii.
13. Matt.
xxvi. 64.
of as the "*Son of Man*" that should
come "*in the clouds of heaven*," but Who
am content, for the time being, to go in
and out as a man amongst men on earth,
—who say they that I am?   "*And they
said, Some say that Thou art John the
Baptist; some, Elias; and others, Jeremias, or one of the prophets.*"   As St.
Mark says, on another occasion, "*The
See chap.
xii. 37.
common people heard Him gladly;*" they
could not but admit that He was one
that was mighty in word and deed, and
a holy person, and going about doing
good.   Herod, as we read elsewhere,
See chap.
xiv. 1, 2.
thought he was John Baptist, others
declared that "*one of the old prophets*"

was "*risen again.*" And thus opinions
were divided, after a then well-known
idea, " that the souls of dead men, according to their several merits, did trans-
migrate into other bodies of very perfect and excellent persons." This reply
made, our Lord then puts the question
to the Apostles generally, "*But whom
say* YE *that I am ?* " Whereupon Peter,
here as elsewhere the ready spokesman
of the rest [4], at once replied, "*Thou art
the Christ, the Son of the living God.*"
Neither John Baptist art Thou, nor
Elias, nor Jeremias, nor *one* of the prophets ; yea, rather that Great Prophet
to whom all these bare testimony—not
simply anointed to Thine office, as
priests, and prophets, and kings were
wont to be anointed—but THE anointed
One of God, " THE *Christ, the Son of the*

Luke ix.
19.

Jer. Tayl.
iii. 190.

---

[4] This is pretty much in the words of St. Chrysostom, who calls Peter ὁ πανταχοῦ θερμὸς, ὁ τοῦ
χοροῦ τῶν ἀποστόλων κορυφαῖος, which, although sometimes objected to, is very near the truth. See Hom.
liv. in loc. Ed. Field, vol. ii. 107. See also Theophylact in loc., and his clear and reasonable remarks on
" THE CHRIST"—μετὰ τοῦ ἄρθρου—ut supra, p. 84. D.

living God"—of that Almighty Lord Who alone of all beings hath life in Himself, and Who giveth life to all that liveth, without beginning and without end, eternal and everlasting, "*the blessed and only Potentate, the King of kings, and Lord of lords.*" Such, in fuller words, was the intent of Peter's confession; and a good confession it was, acknowledging Christ to be "*the honourable, true, and only Son,*" "*the King of Glory,*" "*the everlasting Son of the Father,*" very and true Christ, the anointed One of God, the Messias so long expected !

On which we may observe, that Peter now, and the other Apostles, had had full time to arrive at the sense of their own Scriptures which pointed unto Christ: even as we Christians have had full time to adorn the doctrine of God our Saviour in all things, since we were baptized into Christ. Time is allotted unto us, more or less, as it may be, to work out our "*own salvation with fear and trembling,*" and a ready obedience to

1 Tim. vi. 15.

the revealed Word. And then, after a while, there is a reckoning and a questioning, whereby to know if the talents committed unto us have been properly used. And so it was in the instance before us. For Christ did not put this question at the commencement of His ministry [5], but now, in the third year of it, when He had done many miracles, and had afforded many clear proofs of His Godhead, and of His Oneness with the Father. And sure enough, Christian Brethren, long time, so to say, hath He been going in and out amongst us, and we have had full opportunity ourselves of making a good confession, as Peter did; and of serving our Lord and Saviour by a holy faith, and a holy life, and a willing obedience! The question is, Have we done so? Are we ready to confess Christ, as Peter did, to be our alone God and Saviour? If we be, it is well with us, and "*good words and comfortable words*" Zech. i. 13.

---

[5] St. Chrysostom touches clearly upon this point, which, I think, is material: Διὰ δὴ τοῦτο οὐδ' ἐν ἀρχῇ τοῦ κηρύγματος κ.τ.ἑ. See ut suprà, p. 106. Ed. Field.

shall be uttered to us through our consciences.   For, in as far forth as appertaineth to our everlasting salvation, the
Lord Christ will speak to us in some
sort as He did to Peter.   He will, at
least, assure us that He is " *the way, the
truth, and the life ;*" that they whose faith
is rooted and grounded in Him, shall
never be cast out.   He is *their* rock
Who compared Peter's faithful confess-
sion [6] to the strength of a rock, and gave

---

[6] Though I do not follow the Lutheran and Cal-
vinistic interpretation, I admit it thus far,—in St.
Chrysostom's words referred to Peter, — τουτέστι
τῇ πίστει τῆς ὁμολογίας, p. 108, Field ; or, as in
Theophylact more fully, tom. i. 85. B.   And these are
followed by Jer. Tayl. iii. 191 ; Bp. Reynolds, iii.
337 ; Beveridge on Art. XXXVII. vol. ii. 396 ;
Calvin, Harm. ii. 109 ; August. in Cat. Aur. p. 585 ;
Taverner on Postils, p. 549, Cardwell.
    Since the former part of this note was written,
I observe, on a reperusal of Faber's Difficulties of
Romanism, that St. Chrysostom also explained Peter
to be the Rock.   Which of the two opinions he held
to be the last would be a chronological question of
little import.   See Faber, p. 61, 2nd edit.   I would
wish to refer likewise to a note in the Rev. C. Dodg-
son's Translation of Tertullian, note Q, p. 492, &c.
which contains almost all that can be needed on this
question.   Both interpretations, as Beveridge ro-

him a never-to-be-forgotten name, and honour till the end of time!

But, or ever I proceed to further practical remarks, it will be well to consider our Lord's reply, noting, by the way, that whatever *general* confessions had been made previously as to our Lord's being the Son of God—as, for example, by Nathanael, or by other the Apostles upon the lake of Gennesaret, after the storm—yet, here, and in this passage before us, St. Peter was first and foremost in a confession the most open and the most distinct of the Messiahship of the eternal Son. John i. 49. Matt. xiv. 33.

And hereupon it was that "*Jesus answered and said unto him, Blessed art thou, Simon Bar-Jona, for flesh and blood hath not revealed it unto thee, but My Father which is in heaven.*" Happy son of Jonas, thus to be pronounced blessed by the Lord of Life! Happy to have believed in thine heart, and to

marks, come to one, since each Apostle could be a rock only through faith in that Rock which is Christ.

have confessed with thy mouth a confession so clear, and withal so true as never to be forgotten more! A confession beyond "*flesh and blood*"—beyond, that is, the powers of human reasoning; wrought in thee by the Holy Spirit of the Father, of whom, as now in a more extended sense, are "all holy desires, all good counsels, and all just works." God was in thee, of a truth, Simon Bar-Jona, when thou didst make this avowal! And therefore did thy Lord and ours' add, "*And I say unto thee, That thou art Peter, and upon this rock I will build my Church, and the gates of hell shall not prevail against it;*" thou art a Rock [7], as thy name implies, even that of John i. 43. Cephas or Peter, which, in the stead of Simon, I gave thee at the first,—and upon this rock—upon thee, (notwithstanding thine infirmities as a man and

[7] Almost all that is necessary on this point is to be seen in Note D, in the Appendix to Marsh's Comparative View, 2nd Edition, p. 278, &c. I am inclined to think that I take the same view that Bp. Horsley does. See Serm. vol. i. pp. 189, 190; but he is not quite clear with himself.

thine after-denial of Me,) firm, and un-shaken, and stedfast in thy faith and love, I will build My Church, and the gates of Hades, that is to say, of the grave and of death, shall not prevail against it. In which words (noways ap-plicable, as I hinted before, to Romish notions of Infallibility and Supremacy) you should take notice, that our Saviour, speaking of His Church, "mentioneth it as that which then was not, but after-wards was to be; but when He ascended into heaven, and the Holy Ghost came down, when Peter had converted "*three thousand souls*," which were added to the "*hundred and twenty*" disciples, then was there a Church (and that built upon Peter according to our Saviour's promise); for after that we read, "*The Lord added to the Church daily such as should be saved;*" even as He doth still, and will do: for whosoever, as Peter did, shall confess the Lord Christ from the heart, believing in Him as the only Mediator between God and man, that man certainly shall be called forth from

Isa. xxxiii. 10. Ps. ix. 18.

Pearson on the Creed, ix. i. 506.

out of this naughty world, shall be a corresponding member of the Church of the first-born in Heaven, and shall be consigned over, in God's own good time, to those eternal and abiding mansions, reserved as "*the inheritance of the saints in light.*"

One portion of our Saviour's reply to Peter yet remains, and it is this: "*I will give unto thee the keys of the kingdom of heaven; and whatsoever thou shalt bind on earth shall be bound in heaven; and whatsoever thou shalt loose on earth shall be loosed in heaven,*"—in which words is to be noted the use of "*bind*" and "*loose*" in the teaching of the Rabbis[8], who when they disallowed any thing as unlawful, were said to "*bind*" it; when they pronounced any thing lawful, or permitted it, were said to "*loose*" it. Noted is it to be also, that what was here said to Peter, was elsewhere

---

[8] See the collected passages in Lightfoot's "*Talm. and Hebr. Exercit.*" in loc., and the additions of *Schoetgen*, Ibid. It is hardly necessary to say, that the Hebrew sense of "*bind*" and "*loose*" is the reverse of the Greek. See Commentators, *in loc.*

said to the other Apostles also; from Cf. Matt. xviii. 18, with John xx. 23. which is to be inferred, that his ready and earnest confession on the present occasion, gained him that honour at the mouth of his Lord and his God, which zeal tempered with knowledge so well deserved. Clearly, as we know from the Acts of the Apostles, "*the keys*," were put into his hands, and he opened the doors of the Christian Church to all Jewish and Gentile believers. To him was this honour given as a saint of Christ; but "*such honour*" also had all his saints and Apostles,—even as St. Paul said to the Ephesian converts, We "*are built upon the foundation of the apostles and prophets, Jesus Christ himself being the chief corner-stone.*" Peter, Ephes. ii. 20. or Paul, or other holy men, as pillars of the Church and ambassadors of heaven, by their assured and godly doctrine after "*the truth as it is in Jesus,*" may either "open the gates thereof unto the faithful and penitent, or shut them upon the impenitent, disobedient unbelievers;" Bp. Hall's Par. but mind we this well, "*Other founda-*

H

1 Cor. iii. 11. *tion can no man lay than that is laid, which is Jesus Christ."*

And thus, in very plain words, simply and intelligibly, because it occurred in the lesson for the day, have I endeavoured to explain to you, Christian Brethren, these well-known but. much disputed verses; and I would offer, by way of summing up, the remarks which follow.

I. With reference to the disputes of Rome. It is a very doubtful matter indeed if Peter was ever her bishop [9]. Individually, I am persuaded he never was; though there is little reason to doubt that he died there, and in the same persecution with Paul. And, as to other pretensions, such as his Su-

---

[9] On this point, see authorities in Lardner, c. xviii. St. Peter, § vii. Supplement, vol. iii. p. 189, &c. See also Hammond's "Dissertatio Quinta de omnibus Clementis Rom." &c. vol. iv. 824, 5. Eusebius twice records that he was crucified there. I have before referred to Bp. Pearson's " Dissertationes Duæ de Serie et Successione primorum Romæ Episcoporum." See Minor Theol. Works, vol. ii. 276, &c. Add Faber's Difficulties of Romanism, book i. c. iii. p. 724. 2nd edition.

premacy, and so forth, it may be truly said, as of "Purgatory, Pardons, Worshipping and Adoration as well of Images as of Reliques, and also Invocation of Saints," that "it is a fond thing vainly invented, and grounded upon no warranty of Scripture, but rather repugnant to the Word of God;"—which is all I think it necessary to say upon this head. *See Art. XXII. Purgatory.*

II. The rather, ye Christian people, I do call ye to more practical matters. I do call ye to make a good confession, as Peter did; to hold ye fast by "*Christ and Him crucified,*" and the real sanitory measure of his Cross, which shall save your souls alive in the day of visitation. Whereas, to put your trust in any else—in any child of man—however high, however exalted in his pride of place, is but to work your own ruin and your own fall; "*for there is one God, and one Mediator between God and men, the man Christ Jesus.*" Even *He* who *1 Tim. ii. 5.* condescended to *call* Himself, and to *be,* the Son of Man, though at the same time he was the Son of God from all

H 2

eternity——higher than the heavens, which
he bowed in his incomprehensible humility, sojourning on earth for us men
and for our salvation, who else were lost
ones altogether!

III. Next, I do have ye note, that
the words, " *Blessed art thou, Simon Bar-
Jona*," go on to prophesy to each one of
us.   Not unto Peter alone, but unto
all, everywhere[10], who shall call upon the
name of the Lord, is this blessedness
consigned.   The faithful, like Peter,
shall be " *Rocks*" every where, and in
every land; not, it is true " *Rocks*" like
Christ, who endureth ever; but firm and
solid holds nevertheless, and " *lively
stones*" in the Christian Church.   In St.
Peter's own words, " *To whom coming as
unto a living stone, disallowed indeed of
men, but chosen of God and precious, ye
also, as lively stones, are built up a spiritual house, an holy priesthood, to offer*

[10] Cæterum non uni Petro hoc privatim dixit, sed
ostendere voluit, ubi sita sit unica totius mundi feli-
citas," &c.   See Calvin, Har. Pars Altera, in loc.
Ed. Tholuck, ii. 106.

up spiritual sacrifices, acceptable to God by Jesus Christ." See 1 Pet. ii. 4, 5.

IV. Whosoever they are who, in simplicity and godly sincerity, shall give themselves over unto Christ; not framing systems for themselves, and out of their own heads, but following on to know the Lord, and "*the truth as it is in Jesus,*" who is "*the Christ, the Son of the living God,*"—following on, I say, to know him in holiness and righteousness of life,—*those,* a certain, sure light shall never fail. Their light is Christ, and him alone; and, as the Psalmist said prophetically, long time ago, In *His* "*light*" they shall "*see light,*" who is "*the light of men.*" Sinful as we are, and dark as this world is, "*There is sprung up light for the righteous, and joyful gladness for such as are true-hearted.*" Ps. xxxvi. 9. John i. 4. Ps. xcvii. 11.

V. Lastly, as the Lord said unto Peter, that "*the gates of hell*" should not prevail against his Church,—even so it is with the members of that Church. The "*gates of hell*" shall not prevail against them! Death and destruction

cannot prevail against those that are
Christ's. The fame of His manifesta-
tion in the flesh have they heard with
their ears, and their power is gone!
The bars of the pit are broken, and there
is a huge grave delivery[11]! Christ, who
is the Resurrection and the Life doth
say, and the dead hear his voice in
silence, *" O death, I will be thy plagues :*
O grave, I will be thy destruction !"

See Hosea
xiii. 14.

Of so great avail is it to make a good
confession with Peter—to abide by it—
to cling to the cross, and to say, in life
or in the hour of death, "THOU ART THE
CHRIST, THE SON OF THE LIVING GOD!"

---

[11] " Firmly as the gates of Hades may be barred, they
shall have no power to confine his departed Saints,
when the last trump shall sound, and the voice of the
Archangel shall thunder through the deep." See Bp.
Horsley's Serm. Theol. Works, vol. i. 192.

SERMON III.

ONE MEDIATOR.

" De quo Mediatore longum est, ut quanta dignum est tanta dicantur, quamvis ab homine dici dignè non possint. Quis enim hoc solum congruentibus, explicet verbis quod *Verbum caro factum est et habitavit in nobis*, ut crederemus in Dei Patris Omnipotentis unicum Filium natum de Spiritu Sancto et Mariâ Virgine ! ''—AUGUST. *Enchiridion*, &c. c. xxxiv. tom. vi. 209. *Bened.*

Ὁ Χριστὸς δύο τίνων ἐστὶ μεσίτης, Θεοῦ δηλαδὴ καὶ ἀνθρώπων· ἐμεσίτευσε γὰρ ἀμφοτέροις, εἰρήνην ποιήσας, καὶ τὸν πόλεμον λύσας, ὃς ἦν τοῖς ἀνθρώποις πρὸς Θεόν· ἀφ' οὗ γὰρ ἥνωσεν ἑαυτῷ τὴν ἀνθρωπίνην φύσιν, ἔκτοτε τὴν εἰρήνην ἐποίησε, τῇ θείᾳ φύσει τὴν ἐχθρὰν διὰ τῆς ἁμαρτίας σάρκα παραδόξως ἀνακεράσας. — THEOPHYLACT in Gal. iii. 20, tom. ii. 345. B.

Ἦσάν τινες οἱ λέγοντες, οὐ δεῖ ἡμᾶς διὰ τοῦ Χριστοῦ προσάγεσθαι, ἀλλὰ διὰ τῶν ἀγγέλων· ἐκεῖνο γὰρ μεῖζόν ἐστιν ἢ καθ' ἡμᾶς· διὰ τοῦτο ἄνω καὶ κάτω στρέφει τὰ ὑπὲρ τοῦ Χριστοῦ λεχθέντα αὐτῷ, διὰ τοῦ αἵματος τοῦ σταυροῦ αὐτοῦ κατηλλάγημεν, ὅτι ὑπὲρ ἡμῶν ἔπαθεν, ὅτι ἠγάπησεν ἡμᾶς, κ.τ.ἐ.—CHRYSOST. *Hom.* vii. in Coloss. iii. 18, tom. xi. 372. A.

Ναὶ μὴν ἅγιον ἦν τὸ σῶμα τῆς Μαρίας, οὐ μὴν Θεός· καὶ δὴ παρθένος ἦν ἡ Παρθένος, καὶ τετιμημένη, ἀλλ' οὐκ εἰς προσκύνησιν ἡμῖν δοθεῖσα, ἀλλὰ προσκυνοῦσα τὸν ἐξ αὐτῆς σαρκὶ γεγεννημένον, ἀπὸ οὐρανῶν δὲ ἐκ κόλπων πατρῴων παραγενόμενον. Καὶ διὰ τοῦτο τὸ Εὐαγγέλιον ἐπισφαλίζεται ἡμᾶς, λέγον, αὐτοῦ τοῦ Κυρίου φήσαντος· Ὅτι τί ἐμοὶ καὶ σοί, γύναι; οὔπω ἥκει ἡ ὥρα μου ἵνα ἀπὸ τοῦ, Γύναι, τί ἐμοὶ καὶ σοί ; μή τινες νομίσωσι περισσότερον εἶναι τὴν ἁγίαν Παρθένον, γυναῖκα ταύτην κέκληκεν, ὡς προφητεύων τῶν μελλόντων ἔσεσθαι ἐπὶ τῆς γῆς σχισμάτων τε καὶ αἱρέσεων χάριν· ἵνα μή τινες ὑπερβολῇ θαυμάσαντες τὴν ἁγίαν, εἰς τοῦτο ὑποπέσωσι τῆς αἱρέσεως τὸ ληρολόγημα.—EPIPHAN. *Collyridiani Hæresis*, lxxix. 4, tom. i. 1061. Ed. 1622.

" Nos autem non dico Martyrum relliquias, sed ne solem quidem, et lunam, non Angelos, non Archangelos, non Cherubim, non Seraphim, et omne nomen quod nominatur et in præsenti sæculo et in futuro, colimus et adoramus ; ne serviamus Creaturæ potius quam Creatori, qui est benedictus in sæcula.''—HIERON. *Epist.* cix. *ad Riparium*, tom. i. 719. *Benedict.*

SERMON III.

ONE MEDIATOR.

1 Tim. ii. 5, 6.

" There is one God, and one Mediator between God
and man, the man Christ Jesus, Who gave himself
a ransom for all."

FROM the consideration of the Holy
Scriptures, as our all-sufficient rule of
Faith, without written or unwritten Tradition, we proceeded to the view there
presented to us of "*the House of God,
which is the Church of the living God,*
the pillar and ground of the truth;" and ¹ T
we concluded the matter we then had in 15.
hand, by resting where we had arrived
—that best of resting-places for souls
distressed—that is to say, in the bosom
of "*Jesus, the Mediator of the New*

Heb. xii. 24.

Ps. lxxx. 15.

1 Cor. i. 30.

Covenant." He, Christian Brethren, of God—even the Holy One of God—the Branch that He hath made so strong for Himself—" *is made unto us wisdom, and righteousness, and sanctification, and redemption ;*" in Him, therefore, our peace, our glory, and our trust, we do place all our hopes. Unto us, if single-hearted and confiding, He giveth that peace which the world cannot give. We call upon Him in trouble and He heareth us. What time the storm falleth upon us, He is nigh. It is He that saith, as the Psalmist saw in vision, "*Call upon Me in the time of trouble : so will I hear thee,*

Ps. l. 15.

and thou shalt praise Me." As Himself did say, when manifest in the flesh, as the Son of David, "*Come unto me, all ye that labour and are heavy laden, and I will give you rest. Take my yoke upon you, and learn of me ; for I am meek and lowly in heart ; and ye shall find rest unto your souls. For my yoke is easy, and*

Matt. xi. 28—30.

my burden is light." So spake He, who in all our afflictions was afflicted ; who took off the heavy burden of sin from our shoulders, and bade the oppressed go free! Certain sure, such is the teaching of the Holy Scriptures, and of the Holy Catholic Church, of which we all are members in particular,—undivided, however separate by distance of time and place, if, as regards our "common salvation," we do hold to "*the Faith which was once delivered unto the Saints.*" Certain sure, the text contains Jude v. 3. a blessed truth, "*There is one God, and one Mediator between God and men, the Man Christ Jesus: who gave Himself a ransom for all* [1]." Scripture tells but of one Mediator: of one and no more; not only of redemption, but of intercession also; "for through Him," and Him only, "*we have access by one Spirit unto the* Ephes. ii. *Father,*" and He hath invited us unto 18. Bp. Hall, Himself, without the help of another. "The Old Religion," Now, to the further consideration of xiv. § 2.

[1] The reader is referred to c. vii. part ii. of Scott's Christian Life, for all he can want on this head. The title of the chapter is, "*Of the Majesty of acknowledging Jesus Christ to be the One and only Mediator between God and Man, in order to our truly leading a Christian Life.*" Vol. ii. 226, &c.

this, to us all-blessed, Revelation, (for such knowledge otherwise than by Revelation were too excellent for us, and we could not attend unto it,) the words of the text naturally lead us; and on these we will dwell, in the first place, or ever we proceed to dilate upon other means many, and other modes many, which have been introduced by the corruption of human nature, and the practices of a corrupt Church, to tarnish "*the truth as it is in Jesus,*" and to dethrone (so to say) the Lord Christ, who is God blessed for ever!

And surely holy Job was right when he said, "*How should man be just with God? If he will contend with Him, he* Job ix. 2, 3. *cannot answer Him one of a thousand!*" And the conclusion was good: "*He is not a man, as I am, that I should answer Him, and we should come together in judgment. Neither is there any daysman*" (that is to say, umpire or mediator [2])

---

[2] This is the rendering of the LXX. Εἴθε ἦν ὁ μεσίτης ἡμῶν· on which see Suicer's Thesaurus, with the quotations from Theophylact and Œcumenius in

"*betwixt us, that might lay his hand upon us both.*" Even so was it when this man of Uz, "*perfect and upright, and one that feared God, and eschewed evil,*" spake these words. And, intimation though he had that his "REDEEMER" lived, and that he should "*stand at the latter day upon the earth,*" yet, more or less, was the vision dark, and the prophetic intimation a mystery, till the times of Revelation came in their fulness, and Christ was manifest in the flesh. As St. Paul said to the Romans, this is "*the revelation of the mystery, which was kept secret since the world began, but now is made manifest, and by the Scriptures of the prophets, according to the commandment of the everlasting God, made known to all nations for the obedience of faith.*" Such a thing as this—as Christ manifest in the flesh, "*the Mediator of a better covenant,*"—the heart of man could not

Job ix. 32, 33.

chap. i. 1.

Job xix. 25.

Rom. xvi. 25, 26.

Heb. viii. 6.

loc. Tom. ii. 343. What a debt should we owe to that theologian who would prepare a new, enlarged, and corrected edition of this work, and a similar one of a Latin Patristic Vocabulary !

of itself conceive. God made it known unto the children of men,—lost, and for-lorn, and sold under sin, like bondsmen of a captivity! When judgment was turned away backward, and justice stood afar off, and truth was fallen in the street, Isa. lix. 14. and equity could not enter, matters were come to a sad pass, and beyond the powers of man! *"And the Lord saw it, and it displeased Him that there was no judgment. And He saw that there was no man, and wondered that there was no intercessor: therefore his arm brought salvation unto Him; and His righteous-ness it sustained Him. For He put on righteousness as a breast-plate, and a* Ibid. 15—17. *helmet of salvation upon His head."* Of the Lord's unfailing and unfathomable mercies, when things came to the worst they mended: *" When the enemy "* came in *" like a flood, the Spirit of the Lord "* Ibid. ver. 19. lifted *" up a standard against him."* Man as man could not mediate for a brother man [3]. *" There be some,"* said the Psalm-

---

[3] See Basil in loc. Εἰ δὲ ἄνθρωπος λυτρώσασθαι ἡμᾶς οὐ δύναται, ὁ λυτρωσάμενος ἡμᾶς οὐκ ἄνθρωπος.

ist, " *that put their trust in their goods, and boast themselves in the multitude of their riches. But no man may deliver his brother ; nor make agreement unto God for him ; for it cost more to redeem their souls ; so that he must let that alone for ever ; yea, though he live long and see not the grave.*" Vain, vain ! were such a hope, or such an attempt ! The wise as well as the ignorant and foolish must die, and perish together, unless " DEATH

Ps. xl 6—9.

Tom. i. 181, folio, 1722, and Euthymius ad calcem Theophylact. (Ed. Venet.) Tom. iv. 580. But, perhaps, there is no better reference than to Pearson on the Creed, Art. ii. " It was the law of Moses, that if ' *any one were able he might redeem himself;*' (Lev. xxv. 49.) but this to us was impossible, because absolute obedience in all our actions is due unto God ; and therefore no act of ours can make any satisfaction for the least offence. Another law gave yet more liberty : that ' *he which was sold might be redeemed again ; one of his brethren might redeem him.*' (Ibid. ver. 48.) But this in respect of all the mere sons of men was equally impossible ; because they were all under the same captivity. Nor could they satisfy for others, who were wholly unable to redeem themselves. Wherefore there was no other brother but that Son of Man, which is the Son of God, who was like unto us in all things, sin only excepted, which could work this redemption for us," &c. Vol. i. 119.

Job xxviii.
22.
AND DESTRUCTION." should hear "*the fame*" of one with their ears, greater than themselves and above their power, —of one who could say with authority, "*I will ransom them from the power of the grave; I will redeem them from death; O death, I will be thy plagues; O*
Hos. xiii.
14.
grave, I will be thy destruction."

And, who should be enabled to do this? unto whom should such power be granted?   As before hinted, the Almighty God, seeing there was no intercessor, himself interceded, and undertook for us!   What was pre-determined in the everlasting counsels of the eternal God, for us men and for our salvation, was in so far forth completed, as that the Word which was in the beginning, and was with God, and was God, "*was made flesh, and,*" as St. John says, "*dwelt among us, (and we beheld His glory, the glory as of the only begotten of*
John i.
1. 14.
the Father), full of grace and truth." The eternal and everlasting Son, who was perfect God from all eternity, became perfect Man—even the Son of

Man [4]—in time. And hence : "This we must lay down as the foundation both of our religion in general, and especially of that great Article in it we are now speaking of—that Jesus Christ, the Mediator between God and men, is Himself the Almighty and eternal God." Beveridge, vol. iii. 58.
And to this intent, as it may be proved

[4] St. Cyprian's words are, " Hic Deus noster, hic Christus est, qui Mediator duorum, hominem induit, quem purducat ad Patrem." *De Idolorum Vanitate.* The conclusion of the Treatise is, " Hunc igitur comitamur, hunc sequimur, hunc habemus itineris ducem, lucis principem, salutis autorem, coelum pariter et Patrem quærentibus et credentibus pollicentem. Quod est Christus erimus Christiani, si Christum fuerimus secuti." Routh, *Scrip. Ecclesiast. Opuscula*, pp. 263, 264. Having before quoted some lines from our old poet, Warner, I may add some to the purpose here.

" By only Christ, our Advocate, we to the Father
 pray,
Nor think we saints deceased can our suits to him
 convay :
Howbeit still, most reverently of Saints we think
 and say,

 .   .   .   .

And follow Saints as they did Christ, and leave
 where they transgresse ;
Such and so much, as said, are we : forgive us,
 God, if lesse."
 Albion's England, ix. book, c. lii. p. 236.

I

by most certain warrants of Holy Scripture, we make, like as it were, a confession, in the second Article of our Church : "The Son, which is the Word of the Father, begotten from everlasting of the Father, the very and eternal God, and of one substance with the Father, took man's nature in the womb of the blessed Virgin, of her substance; so that two whole and perfect natures, that is to say, the Godhead and Manhood were joined together in one person, never to be divided, whereof is one Christ, very God and very man; who truly suffered, was crucified, dead and buried, to reconcile His Father to us, and to be a sacrifice, not only for original **Art. II.** guilt, but also for actual sins of men."

And thus, without entering into abstruse and difficult discussion, you do see, in this matter, the grounds of your Faith, no where more clearly expressed than in the words of the Athanasian Creed, which happily is still retained amongst the formularies of our Church. "And the right Faith is, that we believe and confess, that our Lord Jesus Christ, the Son of God, is God and Man : God, of the substance of the Father, begotten before the world ; and Man, of the substance of His mother, born in the world ; perfect God and perfect man ; of a reasonable soul and human flesh subsisting ; equal to the Father as touching His Godhead ; and inferior to the Father as touching His Manhood. Who, although He be God and Man, yet is He not two, but one Christ ; one, not by conversion of the Godhead into flesh, but by taking of the Manhood into God. One altogether ; not by confusion of substance ; but by unity of person. For as the reasonable soul and flesh is one man, so God and Man is one Christ." Of the *" Church of God, which He hath purchased with His own blood "*—even the blood of God himself—He is the alone and sole Mediator. By His Almighty power as God his Manhood was perfected ; and for us men and for our salvation as Man He suffered, who, except as man, could not have known suffering.

Athan. Creed.

Acts x 28.

I 2

And, perfected through sufferings, He abideth our Mediator still, and will abide the "*Mediator of a better cove-* Heb. viii. 6. *nant*" than that of which Moses was Mediator, in virtue of His continuing High Priesthood in the heavens, "*whither,*" as St. Paul applies the words of the Psalmist, "*the forerunner is for us entered, even Jesus, made an high priest* Heb. vi. 20. *for ever after the order of Melchisedec* [5]." As many as have received the Atonement made by Him are blessed—as many as shall receive it are blessed. He, 1 Tim. vi. 15. "*the blessed and only Potentate, the King of kings, and Lord of lords,*" consigneth such to blessedness! For He did offer up Himself to make Atonement for the sins of men; and, by the sacrifice of Himself once made, and as "*a ransom*

---

[5] See Bp. Reynolds on the 110th Psalm, vol. ii. p. 410, &c. I give these striking words: "As God doth more and more reveal Himself, and the righteousness of Christ, unto the soul, so man maketh further progresses from faith to faith. And therefore we should learn everlasting thankfulness unto this our King, that is pleased to be unto us a Melchisedec, a priest to satisfy His Father's justice, and a prince to bestow his own." IBID. p. 416.

for all," in the place of all transgression, actual or original, this second Adam, —"*the Lamb slain from the foundation of the world,*" perfected for ever those that would walk in His most holy steps, and be perfect. He stood between the living and the dead — the only competent and effectual "*days-man,*"—and the plague of death was stayed; and, not only so, but by His effectual aid within us, through the operation of the Holy Spirit of Grace, the body of our sin maketh not head, but becometh tributary to prayer [6], and the prayer of faith in Him who holdeth the "*golden censer*" is accepted—aye! Himself—the Mediator Himself—doth "*offer the prayers of all Saints upon the golden altar which is before the throne.*" And thus, though the time of our trial and probation here on earth be long and

Ἀνθρω-πος — Θεάν-θρωπος·
Rev. xiii. 8.

Numb. xvi. 48.

Rev. viii. 3.

[6] Reader! Hast thou Anth. Farindon's Works? Turn and see what he saith of Effectual Prayer. "Yet, I know not how—the efficacy of his prayer in his daily conversation." Vol. ii. 622. I wish it were not too long to give in full; for the passage speaketh nothing *ex opere operato.*

troublesome, yet, if we be strong in the Faith, looking only unto Him for help in due time of need, the thing is sure: *" That God so loved the world that He gave His only begotten Son, that whosoever believeth in Him should not perish, but have everlasting life ;"* or, as the Evangelist expresseth it in his first epistle : *" If any man sin we have an Advocate with the Father, Jesus Christ the Righteous : and He is the propitiation for our sins, and not for ours only, but also for the sins of the whole world."* Such is our Mediator ! Such our Advocate !

And thus, in a plain way, have I laid before you, that great doctrine of Christ's Mediation for sin and sinners ; that great doctrine [7], I call it, because that " we are justified by Faith only " naturally flows from it, and we do confess to a " wholesome doctrine, and very full of comfort," and opposed entirely to inhe-

Marginal notes:

John iii. 16.

1 John ii. 1, 2.

---

[7] Luther spoke of it as *" Articulus stantis et cadentis Ecclesiæ."* See Barrow's two inimitable Sermons, " Of Justifying Faith" and " Of Justification by Faith," vol. iv. 326, &c., 361, &c.

rent righteousness, (such as the Romanists speak of,) when we assert that "we
are accounted righteous before God,
only for the merit of our Lord and
Saviour Jesus Christ by Faith, and not
for our own works or deservings." And Art. XI.
our answer to those who speak, saying,
—A man can no more be made righteous
by this righteousness, than wise by the
wisdom of another, is this—(though we
are not careful, in general, to refer to
such points, looking only to Christ, our
sin offering, for the great and good God
*" hath made Him to be sin for us, who
knew no sin; that we might be made*
the righteousness of God in Him ;")— 2 Cor. v.
21.
" No man can be made righteous by
the personal righteousness of another,
because it pertains only to one man.
And because the wisdom that is in
one man, is his altogether, wholly,
it cannot be the wisdom of another,—
no more than the health and life of one
body can be the health of another. But
it is otherwise with the righteousness of
Christ. It is His indeed, because it is

inherent in Him as a subject; it is not His alone, but His and ours together, by the tenor of the Covenant of Grace. Christ, as He is a Mediator, is given to every believer as really and truly as land is given from man to man; and with Him are given all things that concern salvation, they being made over by God's free gift, among which is Christ His righteousness. By it therefore, as being a thing of our own, we may be justified before God, and accepted to life everlasting." Observe, a thing of our own, *as a gift*,—not otherwise our own, not *inherent.* So that when we speak of the Atonement and the Mediatorship of Christ, " the meaning is, that nothing that man can do, either by nature or grace, nothing within man concurreth to the act of Justification before God, as any cause thereof, either efficient, material, formal, or final, but Faith alone ; all other gifts and graces, as hope, love, the fear of God, are necessary to salvation, as signs thereof, and consequents of Faith. Nothing in any man concurs

W. Perkins' "Reformed Catholike," vol. i. 562.

as any cause in this work, but Faith alone. And Faith alone is no principal, but only an instrumental cause, whereby we receive, apprehend, and apply Christ and His righteousness for our justification [8]." Of Him and through Him is all that appertaineth unto our everlasting salvation. He cometh between man's sin and the justice of an all-righteous God, and His people are free!

See W. Perkins, ut suprà, p. 565.

But, and if these things be so, Christian Brethren, as they most certainly are, how say some—the Romanists, who would tamper with our Faith—that we

---

[8] Perkins elsewhere says, quoting a remarkable instance, "And indeed the Papists themselves, when death comes, forsake the confidency of their merits, and fly to the mere mercy of God in Christ." Vol. i. 606. Again, vol. i. 606. See also Laud's Conference with Fisher the Jesuit, § 35, II. p. 238. Ed. Cardwell. The instance of Bp. Gardiner is well known. WARNER thus alludes to it :—

"Ye know, I know, that but in Christ may no
    redemption be;
So your great Friend, our GARDINER, on his
    death-bed could agree:
But to the vulgars open not, 'gainst Rome, that
    gap, quoth he."
       ALBION'S ENGLAND, ix. book, c. 49, p. 229.

are to appeal to other advocates, if so be
our prayers may reach the throne of
grace, " *even the mercy seatward ?* " For
such things they do say; such things
they do teach; such things are contained
in their authorized formularies.　For
example, I turn to the Canons and Decrees of the Council of Trent, and to the
Tridentine Catechism, and in these
here and there, I read such sentences as
these: " Careful instruction is to be
given touching the intercession of Saints,
and their invocation ;—the honour to be
paid to relics, and the legitimate use of
images.　Touching the Saints, reigning
together with Christ, for that these offer
their prayers for men to God, it is a
good and a useful thing suppliantly to
invoke their aid ;—an impious thing to
think that they are not to be invoked,
or that their invocation is idolatry, or
interference with the sole and alone Mediatorship of Christ our Lord."—"Unto
the Saints due honour and veneration is
to be imparted; and in our Churches
are to be retained the images of Christ,

Exod.
xxxvii. 9. .

and the Virgin Mother, and other Saints ;"——to which words, although it is added that " we are not to suppose that in them there is any virtue, or divinity, wherefore they should be worshipped ; and that they are not to be worshipped as the Gentiles did worship their idols [9];" ——yet, although these and other palliating words are added, the practical teaching of the Romish Church, or, to say the least, the result of their teaching is, that the people make these images more than " laymen's books [10]," and (to use the words of our Homily) " although it is now commonly said, that they be laymen's books, yet we see they teach no good lesson, nor godliness, but all error

---

[9] What is here said the Reader will find in Sessio xxv. of the Council of Trent, in the Decretum " *De Invocatione, Veneratione, et Reliquiis Sanctorum, et sacris Imaginibus.*" It is specially said, that they who assert that such Invocation and Veneration is opposed to the one Mediatorship of Christ, do "*impiè sentire ;*" but when it is said "*eisque debitum honorem et venerationem impertiendam,*" the unlearned will not discern the line of demarcation, and their priests love to have it so !

[10] This expression originated from the words of Gregory. See Jewel, iii. 247. See the original in Corrie's ed. of the Homilies, pp. 197, 8.

and wickedness." They teach, that is, that honour and worship is not undue to images and relics ; and the invocation of Saints, after their fashion, leads to their adoration. In a word, they are appealed to as mediators, whereas there is but *" one Mediator between God and men, the Man Christ Jesus."* And, to say the truth, how could other words like these be understood,—even though referred, as they talk, to the prototypes [11],—even though the masses in honour of the Saints be not offered to them, but to God alone —how, I say, could such words as these be understood ?—"Their patronage is implored, that they in the heavens would deign to *intercede* for us [12], that by their intercession they would conciliate God."

[11] The words are "*ad prototypa, quæ illæ* (i. e. imagines) *repræsentant,*" and an evident distinction is made between Gentile *idols* and Romish *images.* This distinction without a difference is properly answered in the first part of our " Homily against Peril of Idolatry," " Though some, to blind men's eyes," &c.

[12] The original words are, " Eorum patrocinia implorat : ut ipsi pro nobis *intercedere* dignentur in cœlis, quorum memoriam facimus in terris." See *Sessio* xxii. *caput* iii.

Doubtless, by such forms as these, carried out much further in practice, the people are led away from the Creator to the creature, from the one Mediator, Christ Jesus, to the many mediators devised by the craft and cunningness, not to say the ignorance, of those who had bye ends, full often, to serve, "*supposing that gain is godliness.*" It is not to be denied that the principle was frequently acted upon,—"The people is willing to be deceived, and let them be deceived;" even as they were, aye, almost "*destroyed for lack of knowledge!*" As was, and is, the custom of the multitude, " they followed the received sense of words, notwithstanding any contrary interpretations." They could not unravel such a device as a Mediator of Redemption and a mediator of Intercession [13]; and the result was, that as regarded images and relics, they had a great share of their devotion; for one Lord's Prayer they

1 Tim. vi. 3.

Hos. iv. 6.

Tenison on Idolatry, pp. 192-3.

---

[13] On this head, see Jewel's Defence of the Apology, part ii. Works, vol. v. p. 221, &c.

said, many were their Ave Mary's [14]; and in the stead of calling upon Christ the more earnestly in their time of trouble, like the two poor blind men, " every borough, every town, yea, every village, in a manner, had its proper and peculiar Saint [15]."

Such, Christian Brethren, previous to the Reformation, was the state of things in this land. Great was the ignorance of God's Word, great was the corruption that followed. Though God had, under the law, most strictly for-

Matt. xx. 31.

Jewel, vii. 499.

[14] " It hath been commonly observed as a great blot in the Romish devotions, that they use many *Ave Marias* to one *Pater Noster*. Which collects, by the way, being repeated by them with such careless haste— the jabbering of any thing in an indistinct, heedless way, is by us called *patering*." TENISON, *ut supra*, p. 235. See Jamieson's Scott. Dict. in v. PATTER.

[15] On this point the reader may see some curious instances in the third part of the Homily " Against Peril of Idolatry," and in Jer. Tayl. vol. x. 226. See again Jewel, vol. vii. 188. " Every man had his peculiar Saint on whom he called ; every country was full of chapels ; every chapel full of miracles ; and every miracle full of lies." Also the striking Confession of Romanists themselves in Bp. Bull's Corruptions of the Church of Rome, vol. ii. p. 38.

bidden image worship, yet was the very Cf. Deut. iv. 15—2
commandment tampered with, and men
bowed down before them. They "*became vain in their imaginations*," as others
aforetime, "*and their foolish heart was
darkened.*" The very teachers of the
people, "*professing themselves wise became fools*," and, to all practical intents
and purposes, "*changed the glory of the
uncorruptible God, into an image made* Rom. i.
like to corruptible man." Indeed, but 21—23.
for God's great mercy, those who professed and called themselves Christians
might have again lapsed into idolatry,
and the Christian Church, in part, have
become a house of idols—not Bethel, Hosea iv.
God's house, but Bethaven, the house 15.
of iniquity. Wisely, then, when our
Articles were drawn up, was this
one inserted. "The Romish doctrine
concerning Purgatory, Pardons, worshipping and adoration as well of Images
as of Reliques, and also Invocation of
Saints, is a fond thing vainly invented,
and grounded upon no warranty of Scripture, but rather repugnant to the Word

of God." Words of warning, and words of conciliation too were these; but not to be mistaken words. If the people had been deceived in a Reformed Church they were to be so no more, and Christ was to be acknowledged as the sole and alone Mediator between God and men. Hence too was put forth (in three parts) that memorable Homily against Peril of Idolatry, of which we may say now (without being responsible for syllables and over-wrought expressions), that it "doth contain a godly and wholesome doctrine, and necessary for these times;" —for the very times in which we are now living, and in which we have to lift up once more our voices against the intrusion as well as against the corruptions of the Church of Rome [16].

But having alluded more generally to

[16] On Coloss. ii. 18. see Theodoret, who expressly mentions that the Council of Laodicea forbade the Worshipping Angels. Tom. iii. 855. c. How much less Saints! The reader may see how the Trent Catechism defends the point of Angel Worship in opposition to Rev. xix. 10. xxii. 9. Under the head "*De Cultu et Invocatione Sanctorum.*"

points of "*will-worship*," which trench
upon and undermine the Mediatorship
of Christ, notwithstanding the palliation
of Romish doctors [17], I must, in such a
plain Manual as this, be short; and
therefore I will only touch upon three
more aggravating forms of corruption.
1st. Of Worshipping and Adoration of
Images and Relics. 2nd. Of Mariolatry,
or Worship of the Virgin Mary. 3rd.
Of Invocation of Saints. For to these
the Roman Catholics, more or less, still
cling; and in so doing, as in other matters
hereafter to be referred to, endanger
their existence as a Church.

I. And, first, as regards the WOR-
SHIPPING AND ADORATION OF IMAGES

---

[17] Burnet's words are to the point: "So impossible is it to restrain Superstition, when it has once got
ahead and has prevailed, that, in conclusion, all things
that were asked, either of God or Christ, come to be
asked from the Saints, in the same humility both of
gesture and expression ; in which, if there was any
difference made, it seemed to be rather on the side of
the Blessed Virgin and the Saints." On Art. XXII.
Add to this his striking words (a little before) on the
decent burial of the bodies of the Saints—in the stead
of worshipping their relics.

K

AND RELICS. Nothing of this sort, as admitted by Roman Catholics—and not admitted only, but authorized also—was Jewel, vii. 373. known to the Catholic Church for the space of five hundred years. Look where ye will into ancient ecclesiastical history, and ye will find nothing of the sort. Even as regards the earthly remains of the aged Martyr Polycarp, it is simply said, " We gathered his bones, more precious than pearls [18], and better tried than gold, and buried them in the place that was fit for the purpose, where, God willing, we being gathered together, the Lord will grant that, with joy and gladness, we may celebrate the birthday of His Martyr, both for the remembrance of such as have been crowned before, and also to the preparation and stirring up of such as hereafter shall strive." So find we it written in that

[18] Cf. Euseb. Eccl. Hist. lib. iv. c. 15. Οὕτως τε ἡμεῖς ὕστερον ἀνελόμενοι τὰ τιμιώτερα λίθων πολυτελῶν καὶ δοκιμώτερα ὑπὲρ χρυσίον ὀστᾶ αὐτοῦ, ἀπεθέμεθα ὅπου καὶ ἐκόλουθον ἦν· κ. τ. ἑ. The translation is from the old English version of Meredith Hanmer, now before me, p. 67. Folio, 1585.

early testimony, the Epistle of the Smyrnæans, written upon his martyrdom. At such a time, indeed—a time of danger and dismay—their thoughts were centred upon Christ and Him alone. He was their helper and defender in time of need, neither looked they to any other. Yet, saith the Council of Trent [19], to which the modern Romanist is more or less bound, "the saints, whose similitude these images bear, we

[19] The words are, "Id quod Conciliorum, præsertim verò secundæ Nicænæ Synodi, decretis contra imaginum oppugnatores est sancitum." *Sessio* **xxv.** *ut suprà.* For the canons, &c. of this Council, see Beveridge's Synodicon, vol. i. 284, particularly Canons vii. ix., together with that learned Prelate's " Annotationes" subjoined to the second volume of that most valuable work, p. 165, &c. " Quantâ autem offensione, quantoque odio Ecclesia nostra Britannica decretum præsentis Synodi de adorandis imaginibus tunc temporis excipiebat, Historici nostri, Rogerus Hovedenus, Simeon Dunelmensis, aliique ubertim tradiderunt. A Græcis autem omnibus, non minus quàm ab hodiernis Papistis, Synodus hæc septima Œcumenica habita est, et Canones ab eâ constituti in ipsorum nomocanonem relati ; quo factum est, ut isti etiam inter alios, una cum scholiis suis in hoc opere exhibeantur." *Ibid.* See also Jewel, vol. viii. 90.

K 2

venerate—a truth inculcated against the opposers of image worship by the decrees of Councils, specially by that of Sessio xxv. the Second Nicene Synod." Wherein it is to be observed, that the Romanists A.D. 787. refer to a Council of late date, contra- A.D. 754. dictory to the Council of Constance, and to the still later one which revised the decrees of the second Nicene—that A.D. 794. of Frankfort—a matter which I notice only to show the little hold the Romanists had to enforce a doctrine, or, as they might call it, a Tradition, contrariant to the whole tenor of God's Word, both in the Old and New Testament. Whereto it may be added that, previous to the Second Council of Nice, one of their own Popes, even Gregory the Great [20], declared against such unhallowed worship; so that Council is set against Council, and a Pope is alive

[20] See Homily *ut supra*. " Et quidem quia eas adorari vetuisses, omninò laudavimus," &c., are his words to " Serenus, bishop of Massile." See also Bp. Hall's " *Old Religion*," c. x. vol. ii. p. 22. Folio.

to the absurdity. In the words of our Homily, therefore, using Athanasius [21] as a mouthpiece, "The invention of images came of no good, but of evil; and whatsoever hath an evil beginning can never in any thing be judged good, seeing it is altogether nought."

Against Peril of Idolatry, Part II.

II. AS REGARDS THE WORSHIP OF THE VIRGIN. Now, all Protestants do pay her honour due. They do dwell upon her memory as one whom "*He that is mighty hath magnified*," and whom "*all generations shall call Blessed*." But, beyond this, they step not a whit. They fly not to her to conciliate the God of gods by her intercession, and to prevail with her Son by her power as a mother [22]. In a word, they keep to the

Luke i. 48 49.

---

[21] "Ὅλως ἡ τῶν εἰδώλων εὕρεσις, οὐκ ἀπὸ ἀγαθοῦ, ἀλλ' ἀπὸ κακίας γέγονε. Τὸ δὲ τὴν ἀρχὴν ἔχον κακὴν ἐν οὐδενί ποτε καλὸν κριθείη, ὅλον ὂν φαῦλον. Contra gentes Oratio, i. 7, D. See also Jewel, "Of the Adoration of Images," vol. iii. p. 242.

[22] In allusion to the well-known words, MONSTRA TE ESSE MATREM; and JUBE MATRIS IMPERA tuo delectissimo Filio! Bp. Pearson alludes more particularly to the decided language of Epiphanius, as before quoted in the introductory mottos.

See Pear-
son on the
Creed.
Art. III.
language of the primitive Church. "Let
her be honoured and esteemed, let *Him*
be worshipped and adored." But contrary to all this is the custom of the
Romanists. None with them so great
as Mary—no mediator so powerful!
Her name even has been inserted in the
Psalms [23] in the place of God's; and,
when the "*one God, and the one Mediator between God and men, the man Christ
Jesus*" has been all but practically forgotten, her name has dwelt upon the
tongues of sinful men! And so doth it
dwell still! The authorized worship of
the Virgin Mary is a certain sure snare

[23] No doubt here a Romanist would answer, "The
vagaries of an individual are not to be set down as the
teaching of their Church." Still the fact remains; and
it is well known that Bonaventura inserted her name
in the Psalms, the Te Deum, and the Creed, after the
teaching of St. Athanasius. See Bp. Hall, i. 680, folio;
Jer. Tayl. x. 229; Tenison on Idolatry, pp. 191. 248;
Abp. Secker's Serm. vi. 328. As an accessible book
none is better on this subject than that of the Rev.
J. E. Tyler. (Part iii. c. v. § 3, relates to Bonaventura.)
It is written in a humble and a Christian spirit, in a
conciliatory tone also, and in a very simple style, such
as becomes the scholar and the divine, both of which
the author is most undoubtedly.

to the conscience. Her intercession
with her Son is appealed to rather than
the Son of God Himself. She is appealed to as the "cause of our joy,"
"the gate of Heaven," "the refuge of
sinners," "the Queen of Angels." Scarce
a name of glory but is given to her!
And although the extravagances of individuals are not to be laid to the charge
of the Church to which they belong;
yet the formularies of Rome herself
cannot but lead on the unwary, and
the unthoughtful, and the ignorant, to
such most dangerous error as is only
pardoned by that mercy which endureth
for ever. And the saying is true, "I
know not whether that Blessed Virgin
receive more indignity from her enemies Bp. Hall,
that deny her, or these her flatterers "No Peace
that deify her." And so, without no- with Rome," i.
ticing the order [24] of worship devised by 642, folio.

[24] That is to say, *Latria* to God, *Hyperdulia* to the
Blessed Virgin, *Dulia* to the other Saints. See Perkins, i. 594 ; Burnet and Hey on Art. XXII. They
are memorable words of Abp. Tenison's, " This lieu-
tenancy of Saints, if they do not really hold, their
Church is a very *Roma Subterranea,* and there is no-

Roman Catholics, as regards God and
the Virgin, I pass on to say a short
word on the third point proposed, that
is, on——

III. THE INVOCATION OF SAINTS.
And here, as on the other heads which
have passed under review, the charge is
pretty much the same. For the due
honour and veneration (as the Council
of Trent expresses it) which is paid to
them by the multitude of the people,
deviates,   as   those   know   who   have
lived in Roman Catholic countries, into
the grossest superstition. In fact, the
Saints are prayed to with such purpose
of heart as superstitious votaries can
command, and they are besought many
times   as   perpetual   intercessors   with
God——as enabled to prevail——as powerful by their merits: as all who have
time and opportunity may see for themselves by searching into the formularies

thing of its meaning to be discerned above ground."
P. 211, *ut supra*. Few have taught better how really
to honour Saints than Anthony Farindon. Vol. ii.
1021.

of that most corrupt Church which has once more risen up against us, and as respects which experience will soon show "that the lower the objects of our religious addresses are, the lower will be the turn of our religious sentiments, and the less they will be directed to the all-perfect Being." _{Hey, book iv. Art. XXII. § 20.}

And thus, Christian Brethren, have I also touched in a very plain way, using the very words, oftentimes, of the Romish Formularies, on these flagrant corruptions,—not chargeable on every individual belonging to the Church of Rome; for tens of thousands there are, no doubt, there, pure and undefiled,—but chargeable on that Church as corruptly maintained. And this I have done, studiously avoiding all intricate questions, and laying hold upon such errors as, touching the Mediation of our Lord and Saviour Jesus Christ, were patent and open to the observation of all such as might choose to institute an inquiry. Other errors there are many, connected with the subject before us;

but these I have purposely passed by—
even the service [25], which existed previous to the Reformation of THOMAS A
BECKET, which naturally would interest
many here, and in which this ambitious
churchman, to say the least, was called
upon by the name of "BLESSED THO-
MAS," and the Lord Jesus besought, BY
THE MERITS OF THOMAS, to forgive the
people their trespasses.   Enough to hint
that such things were!

In conclusion, let me entreat ye that
ye admit, no not for an instant, any insidious approaches to the Church of
Rome in this matter.   Let us keep ourselves from idols—from any worship

[25] The Service of Thomas Becket may be seen in
Mr. Tyler's "Primitive Christian Worship," before
quoted, part ii. c. i. § 2, p. 201, &c.   The curious reader
may like to be referred for other matter to R. Brunæus'
"Monomachia S. Thomæ Cantuarensis et Hen. II.
Angl. Regis de Libertate Ecclesiasticâ."   *Col. Agrip-
pinæ*, 1626.

It may not be out of place to add (for the explanation
of so special an allusion) that the so-called "PALACE
OF BECKET" is at West Tarring.   That he visited it
in his progresses is likely enough.   That he introduced our insurpassable FIGS here is as good a Tradition
as any Romanist one—better, perhaps.

save that of God, and of Him through one Mediator. For anyways to call upon the Virgin, or the Saints, as the Romanists do, is to accept Christ's Mediation by halves [26], instead of pleading our right, and preferring our claim through "that vocal blood and those importunate wounds," with the price of which He purchased and obtained our salvation! In Him alone God is "*well pleased!*" 'Tis He that is "*red*" in His "*apparel*"—that "*hath trodden the wine-press alone!*" "*And He was clothed with a vesture dipped in blood; and His name is called* THE WORD OF GOD." To whom else should we go, ye Christian People? No powers that be, nor

Scott's Christian Life, ii. 243.

Matt. iii. 17.

Isa. lxiii. 2, 3.

Rev. xix. 13.

---

[26] The words of Bp. Hall are much to be remembered: "It doth not more belong to the priesthood of Christ, that He offered Himself once for us (a spotless sacrifice) upon the altar of His Cross, than that He daily offers to the Father the incense of our prayers on the altar of heaven. As therefore many sacrifices, so many mediators, plainly seem to put Christ out of office," &c. &c. *No Peace with Rome*, § 20, vol. i. 679, folio. See also Jewel, vol. v. 222—226.

Saint nor Angel, can do as He can do! He only is "*able to save them to the uttermost that come to God by Him, seeing He ever liveth to make intercession for them.*"

Heb. vii. 25.

SERMON IV.

TWO CHRISTIAN SACRAMENTS.—
ERRONEOUS ADDITIONS OF ROME,
&c.

" Si enim sacramenta quamdam similitudinem earum rerum, quarum sacramenta sunt, non haberent, omninò sacramenta non essent. Ex hâc autem similitudine plerumque etiam ipsarum rerum nomina accipiunt."—AUGUST. *Bonifacio Ep.* xcviii. tom. ii. 267.

'Ακούων λουτρὸν ἐκεῖνος, ἁπλῶς ὕδωρ νομίζει· ἐγὼ δὲ οὐ τὸ ὁρώμενον ἁπλῶς βλέπω, ἀλλὰ τὸν τῆς ψυχῆς καθαρμὸν τὸν διὰ τοῦ Πνεύματος· ἐκεῖνος λελοῦσθαί μοι τὸ σῶμα νομίζει μόνον· ἐγὼ δὲ πεπίστευκα ὅτι καὶ ἡ ψυχὴ γέγονε καθαρά τε καὶ ἁγία, καὶ λογίζομαι τὸν τάφον, τὴν ἀνάστασιν, τὸν ἁγιασμὸν, τὴν δικαιοσύνην, τὴν ἀπολύτρωσιν, τὴν υἱοθεσίαν, τὴν κληρονομίαν, τὴν βασιλείαν τῶν οὐρανῶν, τοῦ Πνεύματος τὴν χορηγίαν. οὐ γὰρ τῇ ὄψει κρίνω τὰ φαινόμενα, ἀλλὰ τοῖς ὀφθαλμοῖς τῆς διανοίας.—CHRYSOST. *Hom. VII. Epist. ad* 1 Cor. tom. x. p. 51, D.

" Deus propter impassibilitatem, homo propter passionem. Unus Filius, unus Dominus, &c.—Sicut enim antequam sanctifietur panis, panem nominamus, divinâ autem illum sanctificante gratiâ, mediante sacerdote, liberatus est quidem ab appellatione panis ; dignus autem habitus Dominici corporis appellatione, etiamsi natura panis in ipso permansit, et non duo corpora, sed unum corpus Filii prædicamus."—IBID. *Opus Imperf. in Cæsar. Monachum*, tom. iii. 744, B.

Δῆλος ὁ σκοπὸς τοῖς τὰ θεῖα μεμυημένοις· ἠβουλήθη γὰρ τοὺς τῶν θείων μυστηρίων μεταλαγχάνοντας, μὴ τῇ φύσει τῶν βλεπομένων προσέχειν, ἀλλὰ διὰ τῆς τῶν ὀνομάτων ἐναλλαγῆς πιστεύειν τῇ τῆς χάριτος γεγενημένης μεταβολῇ· ὁ γὰρ δὴ τὸ φύσει σῶμα σῖτον καὶ ἄρτον προσαγορεύσας, καὶ αὖ πάλιν ἑαυτὸν ἄμπελον ὀνομάσας, οὗτος τὰ ὁρώμενα σύμβολα τῇ τοῦ σώματος καὶ αἵματος προσηγορίᾳ τετίμηκεν, οὐ τὴν φύσιν μεταβαλὼν, ἀλλὰ τὴν χάριν τῇ φύσει προστεθεικώς.—THEODORET. *Immat. Dial.* i. tom. iv. 18, A.

" Hoc vero tempore posteaquam resurrectione Domini nostri manifestissimum indicium nostræ libertatis illuxit, nec eorum quidem signorum, quæ jam intelligimus, operatione gravi onerati sumus ; sed quædam pauca pro multis, eademque factu facillima, et intellectu angustissima, et observatione castissima ipse Dominus et Apostolica tradidit Disciplina : sicuti est Baptismi Sacramentum, et celebratio corporis et sanguinis Domini."—AUGUSTIN. *de Doctr. Christ.* lib. iii. c. x. tom. iii. p. 49, C.

SERMON IV.

TWO CHRISTIAN SACRAMENTS.—ERRO-NEOUS ADDITIONS OF ROME, &c.

1 Cor. xii. 13.

" By one Spirit we are all baptized into one body,
whether we be Jews or Gentiles, whether we be bond
or free ; and have been all made to drink into one
Spirit."

HAVING dwelt upon the Holy Scriptures
as our comfort and our joy—upon
Christ's Holy Catholic Church, to which
we are privileged to belong—and upon
the one Mediatorship of our Lord and
Saviour Jesus Christ, as opposed to
Mariolatry, or worship of the Virgin, to
the Invocation of Saints, and other like
errors devised by the naughtiness of
man's heart—we come next to consider

those Sacraments which Christ has ordained in His Church as generally necessary to salvation—"that is, which all men ought to receive who desire to attain salvation ; which is not so to be understood, as if God could not save without them ; but that they are the means instrumental, and ordinary seals, by which God hath promised to convey and assure Christ's merits unto us, and commanded us this way to receive them ; so that wilfully to neglect them, or to want them, when they may be had, is to cast aside God's ordinance."

Bp. NICHOLSON on the Cat., from PERKINS on "The Order of the Causes of Salvation and Damnation," Works, vol. i. 73, folio, 1608.

Now, the Church of Rome doth declare, authoritatively: "Should any one say that the Sacraments of the New Law were not all instituted by Jesus Christ, our Lord; or that there are more or fewer than seven—namely, Baptism, Confirmation, the Eucharist" (or Lord's Supper), "Penance, Extreme Unction, Orders, and Matrimony ; or that any one of these seven is not truly and properly a Sacrament; let him be accursed."

Concil. Trident. Sessio vii. Can. i.

Such is the declaration of the Church of

Rome to which the people must assent, and to which, on oath, the Ministry of that Church must subscribe.

We, on the contrary, as Protestants, and belonging to that pure and apostolical branch of Christ's Holy Catholic Church, established in these kingdoms, acknowledge only two Sacraments to have been ordained by Christ—that is to say, Baptism and the Lord's Supper. Passing by Tradition, written or unwritten, we turn to those Scriptures which we are commanded to search, and which, like the Bereans, we do search " *daily*," to our great and endless comfort, and there we find these two only [1], Acts xvii. 11.

---

[1] " As for the number of them, if they should be considered according to the exact signification of a Sacrament—namely, for the visible signs, expressly commanded in the New Testament, whereunto is annexed the promise of forgiveness of our sin, and of our holiness, and joining in Christ—there be but two ; namely, Baptism and the Lord's Supper."—HOMILY of *Common Prayer and Sacraments.* On the Sacraments in general, the " *Institutiones Hist. Theol.*" of J. Forbes' should be by all means referred to, as containing the fullest stores of information. See p. 441, &c. ; Ed. folio, 1680.

L

in the fuller and appropriate sense of Sacraments, as having, that is, "an outward and visible sign of an inward and spiritual grace given unto us, ordained by Christ Himself, as a means whereby we receive the same (grace), and a pledge to assure us thereof." And hence, taught by the same Holy Scriptures, from which the Romanists would *practically* debar the people, thereby hindering them from seeing the hollowness and the rottenness of *abused Tradition* [2], we arrive at a contrary conclusion, and assert, that " Those five commonly called Sacraments,—that is to say, Confirmation, Penance, Orders, Matrimony, and Extreme Unction, are not to be counted for Sacraments of the Gospel,

Ch. Catech.

----

[2] I say *abused*, because Tradition, in its proper sense, is not rejected by Protestants. As Mr. Palmer says—" In England the supremacy and sufficiency of Scripture was most rightly maintained, not against a Catholic Tradition teaching the *same doctrine as Scripture itself*, and therefore strictly confirmatory of Scripture, but against a Tradition imagined to convey articles of faith *in addition* to those which Scripture contained."—*Treatise on the Church*, Part ii. c. vi., vol. i. 493, &c.

being such as have grown partly of the corrupt following of the Apostles, partly are states of life allowed in the Scriptures: yet have not like nature of Sacraments with Baptism and the Lord's Supper, for that they have not any visible sign or ceremony ordained of God." Therefore, we restrict the sense of _{Art. XXV.} the word Sacrament; not denying at the same time that it hath been widely used in days gone by; and that "in general acception," (to use the words of our Homily of Common Prayer and Sacraments,) "the name of a Sacrament may be attributed to any thing whereby an holy thing is signified [3]." Indeed, as one said, "In the writings of the ancient Fathers, all articles which are peculiar to the Christian Faith, all duties of religion containing that which sense or natural reason cannot of itself discern, _{Hooker, Eccl. Pol.} are most commonly named Sacraments." _{B. v. l. 2.}

---

[3] See Ratramni Liber de Corp. et Sang. Dom. cc., xlv., xlvii. This is not referred to by our Homily; but the passages are very apt for those who would look into the point.

Therefore, I say, we restrict the use of the term, limiting it to the well-known definition—"a visible sign of grace invisible [4]." For, "So as the word Sacrament may be taken (for any holy, significant rite,) there may be as well seventy as seven; so strictly as it may be, and is taken by us, there can no more be seven than seventy."

Bp. HALL, "The Old Religion," c. xv. Jewel, viii. p. 9.

And, these hints thrown out by way of introduction, we may now turn to the words of the text, in which, with the chief of the Fathers [5] of the ancient

[4] "We use," says Jewel, "the same words and definitions that St. Augustine, and other ancient Fathers, and Peter Lombard and Gratian, M. Harding's own Doctors, have used before us." See vol. iii. 3 ; viii. 7. Of a Sign, Augustine says, "Signum est enim res præter speciem, quam ingerit sensibus, aliud aliquid ex se faciens in cogitatione venire."—*De Doctr. Christ.*, lib. ii. c. i. And elsewhere, "Quæ cum ad res divinas pertinent, Sacramenta appellantur."—Ad Marcellin. Epist., tom. ii. 412. And on St. John : "Accedit verbum ad elementum, et fit Sacramentum."—Tom. iii. P. ii. p. 703.

[5] St. Chrysostom's words are clear, for, having said, Τὸ κατασκευάσαν ἡμᾶς ἓν σῶμα γενέσθαι καὶ ἀναγεννῆσαν ἡμᾶς, ἕν ἐστι πνεῦμα· he presently adds, πρὸς τὴν αὐτὴν ἤλθομεν μυσταγωγίαν, τῆς αὐτῆς ἀπολαύομεν τραπέζης. καὶ διὰ τί μὴ εἶπε, τὸ αὐτὸ σῶμα

Church, whose authority we admit of as far as it is worth, we believe allusion is made to the two Sacraments instituted by Christ Himself—that is to say, Baptism and the Supper of the Lord. For, having shown, that however great the variety of Christians—their gifts, their functions, and their powers—they were still but for one end, to make up one body, with Christ the Head of the Christian Church, which He came to redeem and to save;—(as he had before said in the Epistle to the Romans, "*For as we have many members in one body, and all members have not the same office; so we, being many, are one body in Christ, and every one members one of another :*")—the Apostle, I say, having pointed out this to the Corinthians, doth in the text declare, that this unity is clenched by the Christian Sacraments, saying, "*By one*

Rom. xii. 4, 5.

τρεφόμεθα, καὶ τὸ αὐτὸ αἷμα πίνομεν ; ὅτι πνεῦμα εἰπὼν ἀμφότερα ἐδήλωσε, καὶ τὸ αἷμα, καὶ τὴν σάρκα· δι' ἀμφοτέρων γὰρ ἓν πνεῦμα ποτιζόμεθα.—Hom. xxx. in loc. tom. x. 270. B. E. And so pretty much to the same purpose, Theophylact, Theodoret, and Œcumenius in loc.

Spirit, we are all baptized into one body, whether we be Jews or Gentiles, whether we be bond or free ; and have been all made to drink into one Spirit:" in other words : " This oneness of ours may well be seen in those Sacraments which are common to God's Church ; for by one and the same Spirit of God, working with, and by the outward elements, are we baptized into the Communion of one and the same Church, whether we be Jews or Gentiles, bond or free ; and are all made partakers of the same Sacramental cup, and therein of the same blood of Christ by the working of the same Spirit." Such is a comprehensive paraphrase of the passage ; and you here see Baptism and the Lord's Supper only put upon the same footing [6]. Christians,

Bp. Hall's Par. Hard Texts.

---

[6] I may refer once more, by way of illustration, to the words of our old poet, Warner :—

" Baptisme, incorporating us in Christ, and us in one,
　Christ's mystical last Supper, where in signe His
　　death is knowne,
　Be Sacraments, except which twaine, do we accept
　　of none."

　　　ALBION'S ENGLAND, book ix. c. 52, p. 235.

as members of one Body—the Church, for which Christ died—are partakers of both. And, as elsewhere, "*breaking of bread*," is used singly for the whole Sacrament, so here "*drinking*" is in like manner used—a part for the whole— entirely doing away with that "maim of the Eucharist"—the denial of the cup by the Romanists to the people—even if Christ's all-sacred words, DRINK YE ALL OF IT, were clean and quite forgotten ! But on this point I tarry not now to speak, as it will be alluded to by and by under the head of other corruptions, "plainly repugnant to the Word of God." *[margin: Luke xxiv. 35 ; Acts ii. 42. Barrow, vii. 685. Matt. xxvi. 27. Art. XXIV.]*

These remarks made, turn to the Scriptures; acknowledging, as you must acknowledge, that the author of a Sacrament, in the full sense here understood, can be none other than God alone ; or, which is the same thing, for Christ is God, the "*one Mediator between God and men, the Man Christ Jesus*." And, what find ye there ? Certainly, ye who from childhood have known the Holy *[margin: 1 Tim. ii. 5.]*

Scriptures, unchoked and unhampered by man's Tradition, find in them but two Sacraments, comprehending the "outward and visible sign and the inward and spiritual grace," ordained by Christ in His Church: but two which have as well the element as the institution. "In Baptism, the element is water; in the Lord's Supper, bread and wine. Baptism hath the word of institution: '*Teach all nations, baptizing them, in the name of the Father, and of the Son, and of the* *Holy Ghost.*' The Lord's Supper, in like manner, hath the word of institution: '*Do this in remembrance of Me.*' Therefore these two are properly and truly called the Sacraments of the Church, because in them the element is joined to the word, and they take their ordinance of Christ, and be visible signs of invisible grace." Again, what saith the Scripture concerning them as the means of conveying to usward their several graces, and the pledge of assurance? Even thus wise, and in words as plain as plain may be; for, as regards

Matt. xxviii. 19.

Luke xxii. 19.

Bp. JEWEL, "A Treatise of the Sacraments," vol. viii. 8.

our Regeneration, or new birth in Baptism, Jesus answered Nicodemus and said: "*Verily, verily, I say unto thee, Except a man be born of Water and of the Spirit, he cannot enter into the kingdom of God.*" And Paul, that was struck John iii. 5. down by the way, and was afterwards baptized to his glorious office in the Christian Church, declared unto Titus, that after "*the kindness and love of God our Saviour toward man appeared, not by works of righteousness which we have done, but according to His mercy He saved us, by the washing of regeneration, and renewing of the Holy Ghost; which He shed on us abundantly through Jesus Christ our Saviour.*" And then as re-Tit. iii. 4—6. gards the Holy Supper, called the Eucharist, or Thanksgiving[7], inasmuch

---

[7] " The which thing," (*i. e.* the giving of thanks,) " because we ought at this table to solemnize, the godly fathers named it *Eucharistia*, that is, thanksgiving ; as if they should have said, " Now above all other times ye ought to laud and praise God. Now may you behold the matter, the cause, the beginning, and the end of all thanksgiving."—*Homily concerning the Sacrament*, part ii. See SUICER's *Thesaurus* in v. Εὐχαριστία.

as when we receive it, we are most bounden to return thanks; what words can be stronger or more clear than St. Paul's: "*The cup of blessing which we bless, is it not the communion of the blood of Christ? The bread which we break, is it not the communion of the body of Christ?*" Than this, what closer fellowship can there be? what more certain means of incorporation with the Holy One of God? Certainly "He which hath said of the one Sacrament, 'Wash and be clean,' hath said concerning the other likewise, 'Eat and live;'" and blessed to all eternity are they on whom the saving efficacy of these Sacraments doth pass!

But and if this be so, Christian Brethren, we must reverently appreciate and duly lay to heart "the sign or Sacrament of so great a thing[8]" as is Baptism

See 1 Cor. x. 16.

Hooker, Eccl. Pol. v. lxvii. 12.

Art. XXIX.

I may venture to refer to my "*Teaching of the Prayer Book*," p. 70. Fuller says on 1 Cor. xi. 24, "At this day εὐχαριστήσας, He gived thanks, hath christened the whole service of the Eucharist."

[8] I purposely quote these words, as they lead to a consideration of the different senses in which "*Sacra-*

and the Supper of the Lord, neither adding to nor taking from the Saviour's words of institution, which, if we do, we shall have grace for grace, and in the stead of empty ceremonies,—of bare naked signs,—we shall have a well of living water, the food of immortality, the blessedness of the forgiven! Therefore, let us hold to them in their full simplicity; let us consider, as the ancient Fathers expressed the mystery, and that significantly, that these two Sacraments, and these two only, did flow from the wounded side of Christ [9]! Looking closely to the Scriptures, with this intent, and that we may be one with Christ, we shall see "*the vain deceit*" of the Romanists, and how they would lead us astray "*after the Tradition of men, after the rudiments of the world, and not after Christ;*" even Coloss. ii. 8. as they do all those who are sworn to their Creed.

mentum" is used. Hey, on Art. XXV. § 2, speaks of it as "any *emblematical* action of a sacred import."

[9] The saying is originally St. Augustine's. See the passages quoted by Beveridge on Art. XXV. Note, p. 210. Ed. Clar.

I. And first : It will not be so necessary to speak much on the Sacrament of
Baptism, as in it, comparatively, the difference between us is less—confined
pretty much to this one assertion of the
Church of Rome, that in it original sin
is altogether rooted out.   Her words
are these : " If any one denies that by
the grace of our Lord Jesus Christ, which
is conferred in Baptism, the guilt of
original sin is not remitted ; or even
asserts that the whole of that, which has
the true and proper nature of sin, is not
taken away: but says that it is only
clipt, or is not imputed : let him be accursed."   Sufficient answer it is to this
what St. Paul says, as well in his other
Epistles, as in the seventh chapter of his
Epistle to the Romans, where he tells
us that in him, that is, in his flesh,
"dwelleth   no   good   thing."   Indeed,
throughout all his Epistles, he clearly
informs us that " this infection of nature [10] doth remain, yea, in them that

Sessio v^{ta}
de Peccato
Originali.

Rom. vii.
18.

[10] Archbishop Bramhall speaks of Concupiscence
as " that pestilence of the soul, whose cankered blos-

are regenerated." It standeth not in the following of Adam, but is our own fault and our own corruption ! I stop not to speak of that other point, that Baptism of itself doth all great things for us, without the Spirit of God that moveth on these waters ; nor yet is it necessary to dwell on any superstitions relative to the water in itself. It is enough to say that such things are, and that, to a certain extent, they constitute a difference. But, nor one, nor other, is enough to induce us to affirm that the Church of Rome hath not the Sacrament of Baptism in its full and proper force ; and thus, on this point, we escape her anathema. Sure enough, we seek not for difference, but agreement, and journey on together as far as we may in God's holy fear and love ! It is enough to add, " that the value or worthiness of the Sacrament dependeth not of man, but of God. Man pronounceth the word, but God settleth our hearts with grace :

soms are still sprouting up in the most regenerate hearts."—Works, vol. v. 149.

man teacheth or washeth us with water, but God maketh us clean by the Cross of Christ. It is not the minister, but Christ Himself, which is the Lamb of God, that taketh away the sins of the world."

Jewel, viii. 14.

II. And, having thus touched upon the Sacrament of Baptism, we proceed, with the utmost pain, and great unwillingness, to the errors and corruptions with which the Romanists have overlaid the Sacrament of the Lord's Supper; that holy feast of heavenly things in which we may eat and drink abundantly to our soul's health! And great and grievous are these errors—great and grievous these corruptions; so great, so grievous, as almost to unchurch [11] the

---

[11] The reader who should desire to follow up this point should read the several Letters of Bp. Hall, and the Replies, in the second volume of his works, folio, 1634. He pointedly and strongly says, in "*The Reconciler*," "There is no fear nor favour to say that the Church of Rome, under a Christian face, hath an Antichristian heart; overturning that foundation by necessary inferences, which by open profession it avoweth. That face, that profession, those avowed principles are enough to give it claim to a true out-

body that owns and encourages them ; certainly to fix upon her the mark and the charge of idolatry. But the simplest way to clear the untruth, will be first to show what the true doctrine is.

And, simply taken as a plain, truth-loving person would take the words of Christ, what can be more easy ? "*And as they were eating, Jesus took bread and blessed it, and brake it, and gave it to the disciples, and said, Take eat, this is My body* [12]. *And He took the cup, and gave*

ward visibility of a Christian Church ; whiles those damnable inferences are enough to feoffe it in the true style of Heresy and Antichristianism. Now, this Heresy, this Antichristianism makes Rome justly odious and execrable to God, to angels, and men ; but cannot utterly *dischurch it*, whilst those main principles maintain a weak life in that crazy and corrupted body."—p. 61. See also the words of Tillotson, vol. ii. pp. 265-6.

[12] The very simplest and best explanation is given by Cranmer, in his answer to Gardyner : " When Christ called Herod a fox, Judas a devil, Himself a door, a way, a vine, a well, neither He nor the Evangelists expounded these words, nor gave warning to the hearers that He spake in figures : for every man that had any manner of sense or reason, might well perceive that these sentences could not be true in plain form of words as they were spoken. For who so

*thanks, and gave it to them, saying, Drink
ye all of it; For this is My blood of the
New Testament which is shed for many
for the remission of sins. But I say
unto you, I will not drink henceforth of
the fruit of the vine, until that day when
I drink it new with you in My Father's
kingdom.*" Simple words, I say, and
plain, and, unless the mind be warped
or biassed by prejudice, not to be mis-
understood. Whereto if we add the
words in St. Luke, "*This do* [13] *in remembrance of me,*" and the exposition (as I
may call it) of St. Paul in the eleventh
chapter of his first Epistle to the Corinth-

Matt. xxvi. 26—29.

Luke xxii. 19.

vv. 23—28.

ignorant, but he knoweth that a man is not a fox, a
devil, a door, a way, a vine, a well. And so likewise,
when Christ brake the bread, &c. &c."—Works, iii.
83.

[13] The reader will recollect how the Council of
Trent interprets these words, and for what purpose.
It is not at all necessary to agree with Johnson in his
" Unbloody Sacrifice," nor with Hickes in his " Christian Priesthood," on the words τοῦτο ποιεῖτε,—though
ποιεῖν, like *facere*, have a sacrificial sense. Jewel says
this argument was "fashioned out by Master Clitovey,"
i. e. Clichtovæus.—i. 22. And he elsewhere asks,
"What Father or Doctor ever taught, that *hoc facite*
was *hoc sacrificate* ?"—vii. 376.

ians together with those *prophetic* allusions
in the sixth chapter of the Gospel according to St. John, and words such as these—
" *It is the Spirit that quickeneth ; the flesh
profiteth nothing : the words that I speak
unto you, they are Spirit, and they are
life*"—the most unlettered and unlearned ver. 63.
amongst us, by the help of THAT COM-
MON SENSE, WHICH IS AS A GOOD GENIUS
TO SUCH AS ARE NO SCHOLARS, AND NO
ENEMY TO A SOUND FAITH, may readily
comprehend that "the Bread which we
break is a partaking of the Body of
Christ, and likewise the Cup of Blessing
is a partaking of the Blood of Christ ;"
moreover, that they are "given, taken,
and eaten, in the Supper, only after an
heavenly and spiritual manner." And Art. XXVII.
that constant martyr, Cranmer, spake
feelingly and to the purpose when he
said "that our Saviour Christ, although
He be sitting in heaven in equality with
His Father, is our life, strength, food,
and sustenance, Who, by His death,
delivered us from death, and daily
nourisheth and increaseth us to eternal

M

life. And in token hereof He hath prepared bread to be eaten and wine to be drunken of us in His Holy Supper, to put us in remembrance of His said death, and of the celestial feeding, nourishing, increasing, and of all the benefits which we have thereby; which benefits, through faith in the Holy Ghost, are exhibited and given unto all that worthily receive the said Holy Supper. This, the husbandman at his plough, the weaver at his loom, or the wife at her rock [14], can remember, and give thanks to God for the same. This is the very doctrine of the Gospel, with the consent wholly of all the old ecclesiastical doctors, howsoever the Papists, for their pastime, put vizors upon the said doctors, and disguise them in other coats, making a play and mocking of them."

Abp. CRANMER's "Answer to Gardyner," Works, iii. 500. Ed. Jenkyns.

But, it is time to declare to you what the Church of Rome saith, therein insisting upon points which lead to the

[14] *I. e.,* " The staff on which the flax was held when spinning was performed without a wheel."—NARES' *Gloss.* in v.

worshipping of the creature rather than the Creator—in a word, to something so close upon idolatry, as hardly to be separated from it, save by subtle and most ingenious disputants.

Then, in turning to the Council of Trent and the Canons there decided on, we find such statements as these, which, for want of space, I am obliged to give in part only [15]. First and foremost, " the holy Synod," as she calls herself, " teaches, and openly and simply professes, that in the holy propitious Sacrament of the Eucharist, after the consecration of the bread and wine, our Lord Jesus Christ, very God and man, *truly, really, and substantially,* is contained under the appearance of those sensible objects," denouncing with a curse those that shall deny that " the Body and Blood, together with the Soul and

[15] I have omitted to note that all my quotations are made from the Paris and Besançon edition of 1823 ; and I do it here, because, on comparing different authors, I find some difference in the numbering of the *Sessions.* The quotations from the " *Catechismus,*" are from the Paris edition of 1831.

Divinity of our Lord Jesus Christ," is there in the elements so contained. Whereupon, to make their priests themselves Sacrificers [16], was introduced the doctrine of Transubstantiation [17]; and such as denied "that wonderful and singular conversion of the whole sub-

[16] The words I particularly refer to are these— "Novum instituit Pascha, se ipsum ab Ecclesiâ *per Sacerdotes* sub signis visibilibus *immolandum*," &c.— *Sessio* xxii. De Sacrificio Missæ.

[17] The reader should see what Southey says on this Doctrine, in that invaluable chapter (c. x.) headed "View of the Papal System," in "The Book of the Church." No book is better suited to these times! The Romanist will abuse it because it is unanswerable —the envy only and jealousy of *nasute* and cut and thrust ignorance could lead a Protestant to do so. "The great Erasmus," says Jer. Taylor, "who lived and died in the Communion of the Church of Rome, and was as likely as any man of his age to know what he said, gave this testimony in the present question,— 'In synaxi transubstantiationem serò definivit Ecclesia, et re et nomine veteribus ignotam,'" vol. xi. 105. Tillotson, ii. 221. The book of Bertram the Priest should be read by all who would know his thoughts upon the point. There is an accessible reprint of it (*Parker* and *Rivingtons*, 1838), with the Saxon Homily of Ælfric as an Appendix. This Homily testifies to the novelty of such a doctrine in the English Church. See Johnson's Canons, p. 405. New Edit.

stance of bread into the Body, and of the whole substance of wine into the Blood, of our Lord Jesus Christ, the appearances only of bread and wine remaining," were again denounced with a curse. This, moreover, contrary to what Canon ii. I have declared to you, and could have proved by extracts many and multifarious, was declared to be the custom of the Catholic Church; and it is added, that what we call the consecrated elements, that is to say, the creatures of Ibid. Sessio xii. c. v. Canon. vi. cultu latriæ, etiam externo, adorandum. bread and wine, were to be worshipped with that holy worship, openly, and in the face of all men, "which is due to God alone." In these, and in many like words more, all tending to an idolatrous service—all tending to enhance the power of the priesthood, and so, by investing them with an immolating and a sacrificial character, the power of a corrupt Church, doth Rome attempt to deceive the ignorant and the unwary. And here again I must pass by many grievous corruptions as respects the Mass—the name in the Romish Church

for what we call the Communion Service—such as are private Masses, in
which the priest alone was to communicate, and Masses for the dead, and
Massings more I know not how many,
in which Christ, they say, is blood-
lessly [18] sacrificed afresh by the priest,
as once He was upon the altar of His
cross; "for one and the selfsame is
the victim, He the same now offering

[18] There is no objection whatever to the term of the
Fathers when properly used; it is only when impro-
perly used that we object to the terms "*unbloody*" and
"*sacrifice.*" As Bishop Hall says in his " No Peace
with Rome," sect. xix. " That in this sacred Supper
there is a sacrifice (in that sense wherein the Fathers
spoke) none of us ever doubted," &c. Vol. i. 678,
folio. See my " Teaching of the Prayer Book," pp.
62. 76. To which may be added the words of
Jewel, " The bloody oblation of Christ upon the cross
is the very true and only propitiatory sacrifice for the
sins of the world; and, like as in the sacraments of
the old law was expressed the death of Christ that
was to come : even so, in the sacraments of the new
law of the gospel, is expressed the same death of Christ
already past." Vol. iii. 330. " *Of the Sacrifice.*" To
which he adds—having given full quotations from the
Fathers, &c. " I reckon, whoso teacheth this doctrine.
leaveth not the Church of God without a sacrifice."
Ibid. 335. The reader should by all means consult
Mede's " *Christian Sacrifice,*" Works, p. 355, &c. Folio.

Himself by the ministry of the priests, who then offered Himself on the cross, the manner of offering alone being different." In a word, with the Romanists, the Sacrament of the Lord's Supper is made into a true and propitiatory sacrifice, offered day by day, and many times a day, in divers places, for the living and the dead. Whereas, as you and I read in that Holy Book, which is practically denied to the people in the Romish Church, "THIS" the Lord Christ "DID ONCE WHEN HE OFFERED UP HIMSELF." In those other expressive words of St. Paul to the Hebrews, *"Christ is not entered into the holy places made with hands, which are the figures of the true; but into heaven itself, now to appear in the presence of God for us:* NOR YET THAT HE SHOULD OFFER HIMSELF OFTEN, *as the high priest entereth into the holy place every year with blood of others; for then must He often have suffered since the foundation of the world: but now* ONCE, *in the end of the world, hath He appeared to put away sin by the sacrifice of Himself.*

Sessio xxii. c. ii.

Heb. vii. 27.

And as it is appointed unto men once to die, but after this the judgment, so CHRIST WAS ONCE OFFERED *to bear the sins of many ; and unto them that look for Him shall He appear the second time without sin unto salvation.*" And hence, thrusting aside, as naught, Romish Tradition, we assert "Transubstantiation (or the change of the substance of bread and wine) in the Supper of the Lord, cannot be proved by Holy Writ ; but is repugnant to the plain words of Scripture, overthroweth the nature of a Sacrament" (in doing away with the outward sign), "and hath given occasion to many superstitions ;" such as are those processions, where all must fall down and kneel before the Elements, and the elevation of the *Hostia* or *Host,* that every one may see and adore his God, not the Lord Jesus Christ, blessed for ever in the heavens, but a god [19] made by sa-

Heb. ix. 24—28.

Art. XXVIII.

Hey in loc.

[19] All writers refer to the saying of Averroes, from Jewel downwards. I quote it from Tillotson's Discourse against Transubstantiation. "It is a very severe saying of Averroes, the Arabian Philosopher (who

crifice and immolation at the hands of
the priest. And hence, too, in opposition to the real, literal, propitiatory
sacrifice of the Papists, we assert again,
that " the offering of Christ once [20]
made, is that perfect redemption, propitiation, and satisfaction, for all the
sins of the whole world, both original
and actual; and there is none other satisfaction for sin, but that alone. Wherefore the sacrifices of Masses, in the which
it was commonly said, that the priest did
offer Christ for the quick and the dead,
to have remission of pain and guilt, were
blasphemous fables, and dangerous de-

lived after this doctrine was entertained among Christians), and ought to make the Church of Rome blush,
' I have travelled,' says he, ' over the world, and have
found divers sects ; but so sottish a sect or law I never
found, as is the sect of the Christians, because with their
own teeth they devour their God whom they worship.' " Vol. ii. 236.

[20] Very plain are the words of Jewel : " Like as the
prayer that Christ once made, and the doctrine that He
once taught, remain still full and effectual as at the
first ; even so the sacrifice that Christ once made upon
the cross remains still in full force, effectual, and perfect, and endurable for ever." Vol. iii. 349.

Art.
XXXI.

A.D. 740.

A.D. 754.

A.D. 1215.

ceits." The corruption of the human heart was at the bottom of it all; and POPE SELF preceded the cruder notions of Gregory III., which the Council of Constantinople opposed, and was beforehand with the Fourth Lateran, which gave to an indistinct idea a reality and a name [21].

And hereupon if any choose to say we make the Eucharist to be a mere commemoration and a bare memorial, it is one of those invidious [22] terms the

[21] The reader will find this very concisely put in Jewel's " Treatise of the Sacraments," vol. viii. pp. 30, 31. On the Denial of the Doctrine by their own Church, see Tillotson, *ut supra*, p. 202, &c. Cajetan's words are considerable,—and their rejection and erasure by authority!

[22] Jewel's own words, in the Apologia, are altogether to the purpose. " And in speaking thus, we mean not to abase the Lord's Supper, that it is but a cold ceremony only, and nothing to be wrought therein (as many falsely slander as we teach). For we affirm that Christ doth truly and presently give His own self in His sacraments: in baptism, that we may put Him on; and in His supper, that we may eat Him by faith and spirit, and may have everlasting life by His cross and blood. And we say not, this is done slightly and coldly, but effectually and truly." Pt. ii. vol. viii. 295.

Romanists, and some [23] too who are not
Romanists, will ever make use of. On
the contrary, it is the sign and the Sacrament, accompanied with salvation, of
so great a thing, so wrapped up in grace
to usward! And no wonder even if
"a holy excess of speech" hath at any
time burst forth with rapturous warmth!
if men have called that a sacrifice in
itself, which is the token of the true,
real, propitiatory sacrifice on the cross!
So do not we. But made one with
Christ,—made to *"drink into one Spirit,"*
—we hold it to be a blessed memorial,
invisibly working great things on the
faithful. And from hearts established
in this truth—from "the sweet commemoration of our redemption there arises
another sacrifice, the sacrifice of praise,
and from thence a true peace-offering
of the Christian soul." No gross or corporal sacrifice do we offer, but a ghostly
and a spiritual one, when we verily and
indeed communicate. Awfully impressed

Bp. HALL, "The Old Religion," c. vii. § 1.

Bp. HALL, "No Peace with Rome," § xix.

Jewel, viii. 33.

[23] This was, amongst others, the notion of Hoadley.
See Hey on Art. XXVIII. § 13.

with God's everlasting mercies, our souls
are enlarged, our hope increased even as
our faith, and we do know ourselves to
be "very members incorporate [24] in the
mystical body" of the all-holy Son of God,
having obtained "remission of our sins,
and all other benefits of His Passion."

Commn.
Collects.

But, Christian Brethren, besides the
idolatrous service which the Church of
Rome leads her people to offer up,
she maltreateth them also sadly, and
maimeth this blessed Sacrament in denying the Cup of Blessing. I look to the
Council of Trent, and there I find that
the man is pronounced accursed who
shall say that, "by God's precept, or as
of necessity to salvation, all and single

---

[24] In the Homily on "Worthy receiving," &c., the
word "incorporation" is twice used. As to the question of the "Real Presence," as we mean when we use
the term, there is no better Treatise than Jeremy
Taylor's. See vol. ix. Works. Heber. See also Perkins, Of the Creed, vol. i. 313, and his Reformed Catholike, *Ibid.* p. 587. The truth is, we admit the *real*,
but not the *corporal* presence. See Hey on Art.
XXVIII. § 11 ; for the words "verily and indeed,"
§ 20 ; and Laud's Conference with Fisher the Jesuit,
§ 35, III. p. 241. *Ed. Cardwell.*

Christ's faithful ones are obliged to receive under both kinds the most sacred Sacrament of the Eucharist;" or "who shall say that the Holy Catholic Church was not moved by just causes and reasons to communicate the laity, and the clergy even not concerned in the administration, under the one kind of bread alone;" or who, in doing so, shall say "that the Church hath erred." These Sessio xxi. Canon i. 2. things, ye Christian People, do I read and know to be practised in the Church of Rome, though Christ hath said, "DRINK YE ALL OF IT;" though I do Matt. xxvi 27. know also that, for many hundred years, till the time of the Schoolmen, such an unholy question was never mooted. For sure, unholy, most unholy, must it be, to hold back that which Christ ordained as part and parcel of this life-giving sacrament. And indeed, if to break the least of Christ's commands be a grievous sin, as St. Cyprian [25] spake, how great a

[25] His words are, ' Quodsi nec minima de mandatis dominicis licet solvere, quanto magis tam magna, tam grandia, tam ad ipsum dominicæ passionis et nostræ

sin in such a matter as this! Sooth to say, "One of the greatest scandals that was ever given to Christendom, was

A.D. 1414. given by the Council of Constance, which having acknowledged that Christ administered this venerable Sacrament under both kinds of bread and wine, and that in the primitive Church this Sacrament was received of the faithful under both kinds; yet the Council not only condemns them as heretics, and to be punished accordingly, who say it is unlawful to observe the custom and law of giving it in one kind only; but, under pain of excommunication, forbids all priests to communicate the people under

Jer. Tayl. vol. xi. 120. both kinds [26]." It needs not to be re-

redemptionis sacramentum pertinentia fas non est infringere, aut in aliud, quàm quod divinitus institutum sit, *humanâ traditione mutare!*" *Ad Cæcil. Fratrem Epist.* LXXIII. § 11. See Jewel's remark, vol. i. p. 380. To the same purport are the words of "that worthy man, St. Ambrose" (in 1 Cor. xi. 27), quoted in the first part of the Sermon concerning the Sacrament.

[26] The words of our Homily of "Worthy Receiving," &c., should be carefully studied, as almost every word is intended to *tell*; for example, on these two

peated that the Council of Trent followed in the wake of the Council of Constance; and ye will readily understand how keenly the Reformers in this land felt the wickedness of Romanist Traditions, as applied to this matter, when they thus expressed themselves: "The cup of the Lord is not to be denied to the lay-people; for both the parts of the Lord's Sacrament, by Christ's ordinance and commandment, ought to be ministered to all Christian men alike." Art. XXX. The fact is, that as "half a man is no man, so half a sacrament is no sacrament;" and our Reformers, who stood Hall. in the breach of Romish corruptions, and died, many of them, the death, to procure our freedom, saw this well enough. And vain listening is it to

Bp. White apud Bp. Hall.

passages from the first part : " Herein every one of us must be guests, and not gazers ; eaters, and not lookers ; feeding ourselves, and not hiring other to feed for us ; that we may live by our own meat, and not perish for hunger whiles other devour all." And, again, " We must then take heed, lest, of the memory, it be made a sacrifice ; lest, of a communion, it be made a private eating ; *lest, of two parts, we have but one;* lest, applying it for the dead, we lose the fruit that be alive."

those who say that, in this matter, the
essence of the Sacrament is not hurt in
the Dry Communion; or to those, as a
modern Cardinal [27], who speak of the
"use of the cup" as a mere matter of
discipline when refused. Christ, I trow,
was a greater doctor than he!

And thus, as regards Baptism and the
Lord's Supper, have I laid open before
you the errors of the Church of Rome;
not sufficient to unchurch her, but sufficient to show how closely she borders
upon idolatry—how profane she is when
she presumes to hold back behind her
scarlet throne the cup which our Lord
has blessed! Moreover, I would that
ye bear in mind that she will never

---

[27] Cardinal Wiseman, in a letter dated London, Jan.
26th, 1851, who speaks in like manner of "clerical
celibacy." As regards the Denial of the Cup he follows exactly the teaching of the Trent Catechism.
See part ii. LXX. "*Sub utraque specie communicare
solis sacerdotibus licet,*" and LXXI. "*Cur Laicis utriusque
speciei usus non concedatur,*" pp. 203, 204, &c. The
prohibition is by the Law of the *Church*, wherein again
we see how the Romanists call in this Tradition. See
the Rhemists on John vi. 58, and on Gal. iv. 3, with
Fulke's replies.

let go the doctrine of Transubstantiation, lest, by doing so, she confess herself an idolatress, as some of her own children even have feared [28], thereby showing also the vanity of her Traditions, which she foists upon her people. Neither, as I before hinted, forget that it was our denial of Transubstantiation that not only kindled her bitter wrath against us, but those fires of persecution, and those cruel deaths in Smithfield and elsewhere, which Protestants never can think on but with sorrow and tears;—albeit too with thankfulness, for that God taught His constant martyrs, as Paul was taught aforetime, how great things they should suffer for His name! Acts ix. 16. Memorable were those words of Latimer—honest, faithful Latimer! "Be of good comfort, Master Ridley, and play the man. We shall this day light

---

[28] Cassander and Cajetan, and others. The words of Cajetan are much to be remembered. The reader may see them in Bp. Bull's "*Corruptions of the Church of Rome*," Works, vol. ii. 257. Bp. Hall frequently pays an excellent testimony to Cassander;—and so did the Council of Trent, by condemning his works!

"They let out floods of blood to maintain their unbloody sacrifice."—Bp. HACKET, 1st Serm. on the Passion, p. 487.

such a candle, by God's grace, in England, as I trust shall never be put out!" Out it hath not been put, neither shall it be; nor shall the enemy prevail against us, even now, but by our own fault and cowardice!

Time and space preclude my entering upon the mention of those other so-called sacraments of the Romish Church, and for our not receiving which as sacraments she thundereth forth against us her anathema. Of one, of Penance, that is, as connected with very great errors and corruptions, I shall have to speak to you again; of the rest I will only note, in passing, thus much:—1st. CONFIRMATION [29] is a holy, ancient, and apostolic rite, but no sacrament; not instituted by Christ, and wanting the outward and visible sign of the inward and spiritual grace, after the sort that Baptism and the Lord's Supper are invested with them by Christ's institution. And so,

[29] Cf. Hebr. vi. 2. Not the Perfection of Baptism, as some have said, but a ratifying and confirming of the promises then made. See Jewel, viii. 45, 46. 48.

as respects the others: for, 2nd. MAR-
RIAGE [30] is a holy estate, showing forth
the mystical union betwixt Christ and
His Church, and in this sense a sign and
sacrament, but in no other. 3rd. OR-
DERS [31], again, or "the ordering of ministers, hath Christ's visible sign and Homily,
Common
promise; yet it lacks the promise of Prayer and
Sacra-
remission of sin," and is but a heavenly ments.
office, a service in which to show forth
God's praise. 4th. PENANCE [32], also, is
in a like case; for although the Lord
Christ commanded all men every where
to repent; yet no where did He invest
Repentance with the awfulness of a
sacrament, affixing to it either matter,
or form, or sacramental sign. And, last

---

[30] The Romanists translate μυστήριον in Ephes.
v. 32, by "Sacrament." See the Rhemists in loc.
and Fulke's answer. Jewel, iv. 543—619. Especially
p. 551 and p. 606. See also vol. iii. 363, viii. 51, &c.

[31] The evident intent in making Orders a Sacrament
is, as they say, to keep up a connexion between the
ideas of Priesthood and *Sacrifice*, with a view to their
Mass. Art. XXV. § 5. Jewel, viii. 53. 56, 57.

[32] See Jewel, viii. 57—60, 61. 63, and Hey on Art.
ut suprà, § 4, and conclusion of c. iii. book xviii. of
Bingham.

of all, as regards, 5th. EXTREME UNC-
TION [33], certain Romanist doctors themselves confess it to be a mere erroneous
interpretation of two passages of Scripture.   It is in fact, like its fellows,
merely grounded on Tradition.   And I
may sum up all by saying, that " the
septenary number of the sacraments" is
"never so much as mentioned in any
Scripture, or Council, or Creed, or Father,
or ancient author : first devised by Peter
Lombard ; first decreed by Eugenius IV.
A. D. 1439 ; first confirmed by the pro-
vincial Council of Sens, A.D. 1528, and
after by the Council of Trent, A. D.
1547." So that, of all additions of this
sort—mere fictitious sacraments—we
may say, in the words of Ezekiel, " *One
built up a wall, and, lo, others daubed it
with untempered morter.*" It has been
the fashion of the Romanists so to
do !

Margin notes: Mark vi. 13 ; James v. 14.   Abp. Bramhall, i. 55.   Ezek. xiii. 10.

[33] Jewel, ut suprà, pp. 65—70, and Hey, § 7.   The
words of Cajetan in loc. are the best negative in any
commentator, James v. 14.   " Nec ex verbis nec ex
effectu verba hæc loquuntur de sacramentali unctione
extremæ unctionis," &c.

Most unwilling to have dwelt on such points as these. I will add yet one word relative to the administration of those holy sacraments which Christ Himself ordained, and which through Him, and through Him only, are effectual; and it is this: The mere work wrought [34], and the bare receiving of them, profiteth nothing; neither are they hindered, as the Romanists talk, by the intention [35]

[34] On the question "*de opere operato*," the reader is referred to Jewel, iii. 398; Perkins, i. 603; and Bp. Hall, i. 643. It means "*mechanically*," and without the good disposition of the communicant. Hey on Art. XXIX. § 1. The words crossed out from the Articles of 1552 were "Idque non ex opere (ut quidam loquuntur) operato, quæ vox ut peregrina est et sacris literis ignota, sic parit sensum minimè pium, sed admodum superstitiosum." LAMB's *Historical Account*, p. 9, No. 26. See likewise the Rhemists on 1 Cor. xi. 27, John vi. 27, with Fulke's answers. Hey thinks we take the Romanists too strictly, *Ibid.* § 4, and refers to the use of the word "*wrought*" in our Homily. Part i.

[35] The words of the Canon are, "Si quis dixerit in ministris, dum Sacramenta conficiunt et conferunt, non requiri intentionem saltem faciendi, quod facit Ecclesia:—anathema sit," (*Sessio* vii. *Canon* xi.)—than which nothing can be more dangerous! See Burnet's words on Art. XXVI. "They do teach that the intention of him that gives the Sacrament," &c. Hey

of the priest, if he wander and stray from his holy ministration. Simply, they are powerful through God, and in no sense has man the upper hand! And hence, he that receives grace from ordinances so holy "must not thank the minister for his worthiness, but Christ for his goodness; and he that receives no grace must not blame the unwor-thiness of the minister, but the faith-lessness of his own heart."

Beveridge on Art. XXVI.

I pray God I may not have offended in speaking as I have spoken. "*Set a watch, O Lord, before my mouth; and keep the door of my lips. O let not mine heart be inclined to any evil thing; let me not be occupied in ungodly works with the men that work wickedness, lest I eat of such things as please them. Mine eyes look unto Thee, O Lord God; in Thee is my trust, O cast not out my soul.*"

Ps. cxli. 3, 4. 9.

observes, " This idea of what the minister is to intend was delivered by Pope Eugenius, in the Council of Florence, in the year 1439; and, though the Council of Trent adopted it, yet Caterini argued in that Council as a Protestant would now argue." *Ibid.* § 3.

SERMON V.

CONFESSION AND ABSOLUTION.—
THE DOCTRINE OF THE CHURCH, AND
THE ERRORS OF ROME.

"Secunda post naufragium tabula est, culpam simpliciter confiteri."—HIERON. *Ep.* lxxxiv. *ad Pommac. et Ocean.* tom. i. 524. A.

"Quid ergo mihi est cum hominibus, ut audiant confessiones meas, quasi ipsi sanituri sint omnes languores meos ? Curiosum genus ad inquirendam vitam alienam, desidiosum ad corrigendam suam."—AUGUST. *Confess.* lib. x. c. 3, tom. i. 171. D.

Εὐχῆς καὶ ἐξομολογήσεως δεῖ καὶ ἱκετηρίας κ.τ.λ.—CHRYSOST. *de Pœnitent. Hom.* i. tom. ii. 283. A.

Καὶ ἀνθρώποις μὲν πολλάκις ἁμαρτόντες, οὔτε ἐκκαλύψαι τὸ πλημμέλημα ὑπομένομεν αἰσχυνόμενοι καὶ ἐρυθριῶντες, κἂν δὲ ἐκκαλύψωμεν, οὐδὲν καρπωσόμεθα τοσοῦτον· ὅταν δὲ Θεὸς παρακαλῇ, καὶ τῆς καρδίας ἅπτηται, πᾶσα ταχέως φυγαδευθήσεται Σατανικῇ λύπῃ, κ.τ.ἑ.—IBID. *Hom.* iv. *de Pœnit. et Orat.* ii. 302. E.

Ταῦτα οὖν εἰδότες, ἀγαπητοί, ἀεὶ πρὸς τὸν Θεὸν καταφύγωμεν, τὸν καὶ βουλόμενον καὶ δυνάμενον λῦσαι ἡμῶν τὰς συμφοράς· ἀνθρώπους μὲν γὰρ ὅταν δέῃ παρακαλέσαι, καὶ πυλωροῖς ἡμᾶς συντυχεῖν ἀνάγκη πρότερον, καὶ παρασίτους καὶ κόλακας παρακαλέσαι, καὶ ὁδὸν πολλὴν ἀπελθεῖν· ἐπὶ δὲ τοῦ Θεοῦ οὐδὲν τοιοῦτόν ἐστιν, ἀλλὰ χωρὶς μεσίτου (*i. e.* human) παρακαλεῖται, χωρὶς χρημάτων, χωρὶς δαπάνης ἐπινεύει τῇ δεήσει· ἀρκεῖ μόνον βοῆσαι τῇ καρδίᾳ, καὶ δάκρυα προσενέγκαι, καὶ εὐθέως εἰσελθὼν αὐτὸν ἐπισπάσῃ.—IBID. 307. B.

Οὐ λέγω σοι, ἐκπόμπευσον σαυτὸν, οὐδὲ παρὰ τοῖς ἄλλοις κατηγόρησον, ἀλλὰ πείθεσθαι συμβουλεύω τῷ προφήτῃ λέγοντι, Ἀποκάλυψον πρὸς Κύριον τὴν ὁδόν σου (Psalm xxxvii. 5), ἐπὶ τοῦ Θεοῦ ταῦτα ὁμολόγησον, ἐπὶ τοῦ δικαστοῦ ὁμολόγει τὰ ἁμαρτήματα, εὐχόμενος, εἰ καὶ μὴ τῇ γλώττῃ, ἀλλὰ τῇ μνήμῃ, καὶ οὕτως ἀξίου ἐλεηθῆναι.—IBID. *in Epist. ad Hebr.* c. xii. ; *Hom.* xxxi. tom. xii. 289. D.

"Nemo se fallat, nemo se decipiat. Solus Dominus miseresci potest, veniam peccatis, quæ in ipsum commissa sunt, solus potest ille largiri, qui peccata nostra portavit, qui pro nobis doluit, quem Deus tradidit pro peccatis nostris. Homo Deo non potest esse major, nec remittere aut donare indulgentiâ suâ servus potest, quod in Dominum delicto graviore commissum est, ne adhuc lapso et hoc accedat ad crimen, si nesciat esse prædictum : '*Maledictus homo, qui spem habet in homine.*' "—CYPRIAN. *de Lapsis*, c. xvii. *Ed. Goldhorn.*

SERMON V.

CONFESSION AND ABSOLUTION.— THE
DOCTRINE OF THE CHURCH, AND THE
ERRORS OF ROME.

Prov. xxviii. 13.

" He that covereth his sins shall not prosper : but
whoso confesseth and forsaketh them shall have
mercy."

THE Sacraments of the Church, as ordained by Christ Himself, last occupied
our attention—and certain others were
touched upon, rather Offices and Holy
Rites as we think, and as the ancient
Church thought, but which the Romanists, according to their Traditions, have
set down in that number. However,
following in the wake of reverent antiquity, and holding to the Scriptures
only, we pass the septenary number of

Sacraments by——admitting them to be holy and sacramental Rites, but not Sacraments in the same sense as Baptism and the Lord's Supper are; admitting them, so to say, to lowlier rooms, but not to the presence chamber of Christ! In the words of the Homily of Common Prayer and Sacraments: "Although there are retained by the order of the Church of England, besides these two, certain other Rites and Ceremonies about the institution of ministers in the Church; matrimony; confirmation of children, by examining them of their knowledge in the Articles of the Faith, and joining thereto the prayers of the Church for them; and likewise for the visitation of the sick; yet no man ought to take these for Sacraments, in such signification and meaning as the Sacrament of Baptism and the Lord's Supper are; but either for godly states of life, necessary in Christ's Church, and therefore worthy to be set forth by public action and solemnity, by the ministry of the Church; or else judges to be such ordinances as may make for the instruction, comfort, and edification of Christ's Church."

One Sacrament, nevertheless, of the Romanists—inasmuch as they have built upon it the most dangerous superstructure—is not to be passed by without grave heed and weighty consideration; I mean that of PENANCE, the Mother of Pardons, or Indulgences, and the near kinsman of Purgatory, and, as such, the stronghold of the Supremacy of Priestcraft also; I might say, of the so-claimed Supremacy and Infallibility of the Romish Church, which, "like the two sides of an arch, naturally uphold each other [1]." And, coupled with Penance, we shall have to take a view also of what, one way or another, is connected with it —of Contrition, Attrition, Satisfaction, Ant. Farindon's Serm. ii. p. 630.

[1] I have great satisfaction in referring here to a very useful little book, by Professor R. Hussey, "The Rise of the Papal Power traced in Three Lectures." It contains, in a small compass, all that is necessary on this head. As I have just been reading over the Sermons of Leo the Great, I may also refer to them as indicative of the manner in which he pushed the Supremacy of Peter,—with no "little horn!"

Auricular Confession, and Absolution, as abused by those who call us *heretics*, for that we *protest* against any teaching which trenches upon the one and alone Mediatorship of the Lord Jesus, " *Who* 1 Tim. ii. 6. *gave Himself a ransom for all.*"

But, in the first instance, we must not allow an unhallowed *abuse* to supersede the holy *use* of what, in itself, and under God's guidance, is of the utmost comfort to sin-stricken souls, who tender the " *sacrifices of a broken spirit,*" of " *a broken* Isa. li. 17. *and a contrite heart ;*" that is to say, we must not make light of Confession unto Almighty God,—of such Confession as He requires at the hands of all such as would make a clean breast of it, and receive the Absolution which, in His name, declaratively and ministerially [2],

[2] See the remarkable words of St. Ambrose, in Jeremy Taylor's " Dissuasive," &c., which affirm " the Priest's power of pardoning sins to be wholly ministerial and optative, or by way of prayer." Pt. ii. § 11. *Of the Imposing Auricular Confession upon Conscience, without Authority from God.* Vol. xi. 254. In this sense we may say, as Sparrow words it in his " Rationale," " When therefore the Priest absolves God absolves, if we be truly penitent." THE ABSOLUTION. And cer-

the Church is empowered to grant, as an underworker in the ministry of reconciliation. Nor, indeed, will the ministrations of the Church, to which you are privileged to belong, allow you to forget this; for, in the Daily Service, when the General Confession has been made, the Absolution, or Remission of Sins, is set forth evidently for such as can receive it; and you are told, even as the Scriptures teach, that the Almighty God hath given power and commandment to His Ministers to declare and pronounce to His people, being penitent, this same merciful dispensation;—" HE pardoneth and absolveth all them that truly repent, and unfeignedly believe His Holy Gos-

---

tainly, as applied to uninspired men now, the words in St. John can scarcely have any other appropriate meaning—" *Whose soever sins ye remit*," &c. (John xx. 23), unless restricted to the Baptismal Covenant. At the same time we must remember what Pearson says : " The Church of God, in which *remission of sin* is preached, doth not only promise it at first by the laver of regeneration, but afterwards also upon the virtue of repentance ; and to deny the Church this power of Absolution is the heresy of Novatian."—*On the Creed*, Art. IX.

pel." And the conclusion is evident, that the Priest hath no proper judicial power, but that he speaketh in God's name. In fact, " the ancients challenged no power on this matter, but that which was purely ministerial ; leaving the absolute, sovereign, independent, and invincible power only to God." HIS property is always to have mercy : to HIM only it appertaineth to forgive sins !

Then, thus impressed, let us look to the text : "*He that covereth his sins shall not prosper ; but whoso confesseth and forsaketh them shall have mercy.*" Which words, it must be acknowledged, are clear enough, and plain enough, and the natural inference is, that there is " but one repentance, and that common to all men without exception, and to be practised in every part of our lives for the necessary mortification of sin." Even as St. Paul testified, "*both to the Jews and also to the Greeks, repentance towards God, and Faith towards our Lord Jesus Christ.*" Such is the doctrine according to godliness—such the condi-

Bingham, book xix. § 1.

Perkins' Reformed Catholike, i. 608.

Acts xx. 21.

tion of the New Covenant. He that
will have his soul to prosper must repent.
Whoso doth repent, verily and truly,
shall enter into life. Christ's atoning
blood hath washed out his sin, and it
shall be had no more in remembrance.
As far as punishment in another world
is concerned, it is clean blotted out—
taken out of the way, numbered with
forgotten things !

But though this be the gracious dispensation of God, reconciling the world
unto Himself in Jesus Christ, Repentance must be so understood as God hath
willed. Unto Him all things are open,
and He seeth and trieth the hearts of
men ; and, therefore, to " *cover* " a sin is
like as though a man should declare that
He was not an all-wise and an all-seeing
God. No prosperity, but loss and
damage, must needs attend such double
dealing ! But if a man " *confess and
forsake* " his evil ways [3], what then ?

[3] The old definition of Repentance by Gregory
the Great is—" Pœnitentiam quippe agere, est et per-
petrata mala plangere, et plangenda non perpetrare."

He giveth the best proof that he can of change in heart and mind; and the great God of mercies and forgiveness worketh in him more grace, and doth for him what himself could not do—maketh him to run in the way of His commandments, and, in the inner man, to delight in that law which his corrupt nature had transgressed. And, in such a change of life we have—(a work of grace, mind, all the while)—that which the Scripture intendeth by Repentance. And when John Baptist preached in the wilderness of Judæa, and said, "*Repent ye : for the kingdom of heaven is at hand*," he bid none do penance [4], as the Romanists

Matt. iii. 2.

In Evangel. Hom. xxxiv. Op. tom. i. 1609. C. I give them as quoted in the new edition of Bramball (iv. 359), not having the original at hand.

[4] Hear Bp. Marsh's words: " The word μετανοεῖτε, used by John the Baptist in the third chapter of St. Matthew, which signifies simply *Repent*, is found by the light of Tradition to mean, ' Do *Penance.*' Hence μετανοεῖτε is so translated in the Rhemish Testament, which is the English version used by the Romanists in this country ; and this translation is accompanied by the following note on the word ' Penance ' :—' Which word, according to the use of the Scriptures and the *holy Fathers*, does not only signify repentance and

talk, but He exhorted all that come unto Him to break off their former evil courses, to seek after God that their souls might live; in a word, to testify a change of heart correspondent to that great change which Christ was about to work in the children of disobedience. Simply, he that would come within the borders of the Covenant of Mercy, and have his soul to prosper, must hele [5] up iniquity no more in his heart of hearts, but confess it and forsake it—do "those duties of the moral law, which must be done, not because they are means to satisfy God's justice for man's sin, but because they are fruits of that faith and repentance which lies in the heart," renewed by grace,—fruits answerable to amendment of life. Perkins, ut suprà, p. 573.

And thus we see the first thing to be looked to by the returning penitent,— even the mercy of God, who receiveth

amendment of life, but also punishing past sins, by fasting and such like *penitential exercises.*'"—*Comparative View*, c. ii. p. 31.

[5] *I. e.*, cover up. A local sense of the old Anglo-Saxon word *helan.*

O

those who have erred and strayed from the right way,—on the conditions He hath laid down, the conditions of the New Covenant sealed in the all-precious blood of our Lord and Saviour Jesus Christ. None, who do so come unto Him, are repulsed as unworthy. If they confess their sin, and as a proof that their confession is true, forsake what they have done amiss, the worthiness of His Son countervails the unworthiness of themselves, which is now unto them the great grief and sorrow of their hearts,—under which their very hearts would break, but for that mercy which endureth for ever, and rains down comfort and benediction on the transgressors out of heaven! Never music [6] fell so soft and sweet on mortal ear as those words of our blessed Lord, " *Son, be of* Matt. ix. 2. *good cheer, thy sins be forgiven thee!* " Yet, unto us, Christian Brethren, if we

---

[6] See Pearson on the Creed, Art. IX.: " The year of release, the year of jubilee, was a time of public joy, and there is no voice like that, *Thy sins are forgiven thee,*" &c.

stop not our ears, hath that sound come.
The same "FORGIVENESS OF SINS," on
our hearty repentance, is an Article of
our Creed consigned over to us [7]. God
is ever nigh, overshadowing us with
mercies! Of Himself, and in the person of the Lord Christ, He summoneth
us all unto Him, apart from other helps
or mediators. He saith, "*Seek ye the
Lord while He may be found ; call ye
upon Him while He is near : Let the
wicked forsake his way, and the unrighteous man his thoughts ; let him return unto
the Lord, and He will have mercy upon
him ; and to our God, and He will abundantly pardon.*" And never is the ex- Isa. lv. 6,7.
hortation out of place : "*Repent ye therefore, and be converted, that your sins may
be blotted out, when the times of refreshing*

---

[7] Hear the words of the great Basil on Psalm
xxxiii. :—Συντριμμὸς δὲ καρδίας ἐστὶν ὁ ἀφανισμὸς τῶν
ἀνθρωπίνων λογισμῶν· ὁ καταφρονήσας γὰρ τῇδε, καὶ
ἀποδεδωκὼς ἑαυτὸν τῷ λόγῳ τοῦ Θεοῦ, καὶ ἐμπαρέχων
ἑαυτοῦ τὸ ἡγεμονικὸν τοῖς ὑπὲρ ἄνθρωπον καὶ θειοτέροις
νοήμασιν, οὗτος ἂν εἴη ὁ συντετριμμένην ἔχων τὴν καρ-
δίαν, καὶ ποιήσας αὐτὴν θυσίαν οὐκ ἐξουδενωμένην ὑπὸ
τοῦ Κυρίου.—Tom. i. 155. D.

*shall come from the presence of the Lord;
and He shall send Jesus Christ, which
before was preached unto you: Whom
the heaven must receive until the times of
restitution of all things, which God hath
spoken by the mouth of all His holy prophets since the world began."*

Acts iii.
19—21.

Look where ye will throughout the
Scriptures of the New Testament, and
this and the like to it, ye will find to be
the summons. God doth call ye unto
Himself, through the Son of His love,
our Lord and Saviour Jesus Christ.
Look to the formularies of your Church,
and you find the like summons. All
men every where are called to repent,—
but in Christ's name! Confession and
repentance have their full and proper
due,—but Christ is not "thrust out of
the chair, from Whose grace they flow,
from Whose acceptation they have their
efficacy!" Even in that most striking,
and holy, and humiliating service—the
Commination — the same truths are
strictly and straitly inculcated, and
the prayers prayed may be summed up

Abp.
Bramhall,
v. 158.

in one: "O Lord, we beseech THEE, mercifully hear our prayers, and spare all those who confess their sins unto Thee; that they whose consciences by sin are accused, by Thy merciful pardon may be absolved: through Jesus Christ our Lord." Unto the God of Gods doth each man put up his prayer through the one and only Mediator! He, without any other aid, is appealed to, to bless us and to keep us,—to lift up the light of His countenance upon us, and to give us peace, now and for evermore!

And this plain, simple confession of our sins unto God, through our alone Mediator, is to be mainly noted,—because, however great the comfort and consolation to be permitted to take off our heavy pack, and to confess to the appointed ministry of the Gospel, yet to confess unto men, even unto men ordained for purposes of reconciliation, —is no condition, under ordinary circumstances, of forgiveness [8]. And the

[8] See the words of St. Jerome on Matt. xvi. 19. He clearly intimates that, in his day Sacerdotal power

Psalmist was surely right when God's hand was "*heavy*" upon him, and his "*moisture*" was "*like the drought in summer.*" For he looked unto the heavens, from whence came his help, and said, "*I will acknowledge my sin unto Thee, and mine unrighteousness have I not hid. I said, I will confess my sins unto the Lord, and so Thou forgavest the wickedness of my sin.*" And such texts as these are to the purpose. "*Return, ye backsliding children, and I will heal your backslidings. Behold we come unto Thee, for Thou art the Lord our God.*" "*To the Lord our God belong mercies and forgiveness, though we have rebelled against Him.*" "*God be merciful to me a sinner!*" And thus, retaining within our Church all the real benefits of Confession and Absolution, as any may see for themselves in the Daily Service, the Com-

Ps. xxxii. 5, 6.

Jer. iii. 22.

Dan. x. 9.
Luke xviii. 13.

was grasped at, when he says—"Quum apud Deum non sententia Sacerdotum, sed reorum vita quæratur.—Hic alligat vel solvit Episcopus et Presbyter, non eos qui insontes sunt vel noxii ; sed pro officio suo, quum peccatorum audierit varietates, scit qui ligandus sit, quique solvendus."—Tom. vii. 124-5.

munion, and the Service for the Visitation of the Sick—we bid each man call upon his God for help in this matter. As above hinted, " None can forgive sins but God only—that is, with an absolute and sovereign power. And therefore the power of Absolution in the Church is purely ministerial, and consists in the due exercise and application of those means, in the ordinary use of which God is pleased to remit sins ; using the ministry of His servants, as stewards of His mysteries, in the external dispensation of them ; but Himself conferring the internal grace, or gift of remission, by the operation of His Spirit only upon the worthy receivers[9]." In itself, the bare *work wrought* availeth not. Heart and

See Bingham, book xix. c. i. § 1.

---

[9] The words of our great divines are not to be mistaken on this head ; for example, those of Abp. Bramhall : " God remits sovereignly, imperially, primitively, absolutely ; the Priest's power is derivative, delegate, dependent, ministerial, conditional."—Vol. v. 214. See also Hey on Art. XXV. § 4. Perkins on Jude, —" The keys are not given to ministers to pardon men *properly*, but *ministerially* to pronounce and declare that God in heaven doth pardon them."—Vol. iii. 497. See also on " *Binding and Loosing*," p. 502.

mind must go together. As a great
worthy saith: "Really to effect the re-
moval or continuance of sin in the soul
of any offender, is no priestly act, but a
work which far exceedeth their ability.
The act of sin God alone remitteth, in
that His purpose is never to take it to
account, or to lay it unto men's charge;
the stain He washeth out by the sancti-
fying grace of His Spirit; and concerning the punishment of sin, as none else
hath power to cast body and soul into
hell-fire, so none power to deliver either
besides Him."

Hooker,
Eccl. Pol.
book vi.
c. vi. § 6. 8.

Such is the doctrine of our Church;
and not of our particular Church only;
but the doctrine of the Holy Catholic
Church, save and except where it is corrupted by man's devices, and by that
desire for pre-eminence which is incon-
sistent with the simplicity of the everlasting Gospel. And to this corrupted
state of a holy ordinance I must now call
your attention.

I. First, then, as regards the "princi-
palest part," as one calls it, of the minis-

terial office, which is to preach repentance, that so we may amend our lives, and be converted unto God,—this the Romanists have changed into PENANCE, and have made it into a Sacrament, contrary altogether to the teaching of the ancient Church[10], and altogether with the view of enhancing their own power as a body, and elevating the Priesthood. Whereas, properly considered, Christ is the great High Priest of the Church, and the duty of the ministry is faithfully to do His bidding,—to "*take heed to the ministry which*" they have "*received* IN THE LORD," that they "*fulfil it.*" To seek high things for themselves is not their business,—the rather is it to "*keep knowledge,*" to seek the law and to main-

Jewel, viii. 57.

Coloss. iv. 17.

---

[10] Here, as usual, the Romanists, when driven hard, fall back upon Tradition. Jewel, having alleged the authorities of Chrysostom, Augustine, Ambrose, &c. &c., against Auricular Confession, "enwrapped," as Hooker expresses it, "within the folds and plaits" of Penance, as a Sacrament, quotes the Gloss. upon the Decrees to that intent—"*Melius dicitur confessionem institutam fuisse à quadam universalis ecclesiæ Traditione, potius quam ex Novi vel Veteris Testamenti authoritate.*"—See vol. iv. 529; viii. 62.

Mal. ii. 7.
Rom. xii.
16.

tain the testimony "*as the messenger of the Lord of Hosts,*" and to "*condescend to men of low estate.*" In a word, it appertained not to the Priest's office to institute Sacraments, but having received those which the Lord had ordained, so to administer them as that they should lose none of their saving effects, even if that were possible, by passing through mortal hands, and the conduit of an earthen vessel !

This, however, as appertained to Penance, was unthought on, and human aggrandizement, not humiliation, was uppermost. The Priest sought great things for himself and for his order ; and that change or renovation of mind, which Christ had made a necessary condition of the New Covenant, after the lapse of hundreds of years, was declared to be a Sacrament, dependent on the power of the Keys [11], as it was called, which Keys

[11] In itself, the " Power of the Keys," legitimately used, is altogether unobjectionable,—nay, committed to the Priesthood,—but rather " to open than to shut," as Jewel observes, quoting the words of St. Chrysostom. *Opus Imperfect. in Matt.* Hom. xliv.

were in the hands of the Priesthood, who alone could bind or loose, open or shut.

But, as I said, nothing of this sort was known to the early Church. It was by degrees that corruption crept in—noiselessly and softly like the tide on a leeshore. Creep in, however, it did, and when once "*Repentance toward God, and Faith towards our Lord Jesus Christ,*" was invested with Sacramental trappings, ignorance without, and the cunning sleight of priestly power within the Roman Catholic Church, especially, was the means of subjecting men's minds to the lowest degradation [12]. They sought forgiveness at the hands of their priests

He only adduces the latter part ; I give it in full : " Clavicularii autem sunt sacerdotes, quibus creditum est verbum docendi et interpretandi Scripturas. Clavis autem est verbum scientiæ Scripturarum, per quam aperitur hominibus janua veritatis. Adapertio autem est interpretatio vera."—Tom. vi. clxxxvi. in Append. See Jewel, vol. ii. 118.

[12] Bp. Hall quaintly says of forced Sacramental Confession, " This bird was hatched in the Council of Lateran, A.D. 1215 ; fully plumed in the Council of Trent ; and now lately hath her feathers dressed by the modern Casuists." See " The Old Religion," c. xiii.

—not through Christ. They saw not,—the more so because the Scriptures were a sealed Book,—that this forgiveness had God for its Author, and that man was but "a co-operator, by Him assigned to work for, with, and under Him." And thus it has come about, that whereas with us of the Protestant Church, "the remission of sins is ascribed to God as a thing which proceedeth from Him only, and presently followeth upon the virtue of true repentance appearing in man; that which we attribute to the virtue, they do not only impute to the sacrament of repentance, but having made repentance a sacrament, and thinking of sacraments as they do, they are enforced to make the ministry of His priests and their absolution a cause of that which the sole omnipotency of God worketh."

Hooker, Eccl. Pol. book vi. c. vi. § 12.

But, further yet, it was not private confession, but public, and in the face of the congregation, which was the custom of the primitive Church,—as may be seen in the introduction to the Commination Service. Private Confession, in fact, as

a command of God, was never insisted
on for nine hundred years or more after
Christ,—not determined on for some
three hundred more still,—that is to
say, in the fourth Lateran, by Inno-
cent III. [13]   As a great light of our ᴀ.ᴅ. 1215.
Church expresses it, "That the priests
should hear the private confessions
of the people, and listen to their
whisperings; that every man should be
bound to their" (that is, the Romanist's)
"Auricular Confession; it is no commandment or ordinance of God; it is devised
and established by men, and was lately
confirmed by Innocentius the Third.

[13] Hooker's words are to the purpose : "They are
men that would seem to honour antiquity, and none
more to depend upon the reverend judgment thereof.
I dare boldly affirm, that for many hundred years
after Christ the Fathers held no such opinion; they
did not gather by our Saviour's words any such necessity of taking the priests' absolution from sin by
secret (as they now term it) sacramental confession :
public confession they thought necessary by way of
discipline, not private confession, as in the nature of a
sacrament, necessary." Eccl. Pol. vi. c. iv. § 6.   The
reader should refer to the words of Cajetan on James
v. 16, and to a good plain summary in Tillotson's
clxth Sermon, vol. v. 3822, &c.

The Church of God, in the time of our elder fathers, was not tied to any such necessity."

Jewel, viii. 61.

These statements made, I shall now lay before you the very different doctrine insisted on by the Roman Catholic Church,—of which I may say, as has been said of the purgatorial state, that "human policy never invented a more powerful engine for the arbitrary government of mankind [14]."

II. And the Romanist doctrine is this: "If any one shall say that Penance is not, in the Catholic Church, truly and properly a sacrament, instituted by Christ our Lord, whereby to reconcile the faithful to God, as often as they fall into sin after Baptism,—let him be accursed." "If any one shall deny that, for the full and perfect remission of sins, three acts are required in the penitent, the matter as it were of the sacrament of Penance, that is to say, Contrition,

Sessio xxiv. Canon i.

[14] See Sharon Turner's Hist. of England, "Origin of the Ecclesiastical System of England," vol. v. c. i. 55, 3rd edit.

Confession, and Satisfaction, which are called the three parts of Penance, &c.— let him be accursed." "If any one shall Canon iii. deny sacramental Confession to be instituted by right divine, or as not necessary to salvation; or shall say that the custom of secret Confession to the priest alone, which the Catholic Church hath from the beginning always observed, and still observes, is contrary to the institution and command of Christ, and is an invention of men,—let him be accursed." Again, in another canon, it is Canon vi. exacted under pain of curse, that even "secret sins, and those against the two last precepts of the Decalogue," by which they mean the tenth Commandment, which oftentimes they divide into two, "together with the *circumstances*, must also be confessed," and that "once at Canon vii. least in the year," according to the constitution of the great Council of the Lateran. To which they add, "He that saith that Sacramental Absolution of the priest is not a judicial act, but a bare ministration of pronouncing and declaring that sins are remitted to the person confessing, provided only he believe himself to be absolved, &c.—let him be accursed [15]." These, and many more like doctrinal statements are those of the Romish Church. And, when we look for a sacrament under the name of Penance, we find none, according to Christ's ordinance—no outward and visible sign of an inward and spiritual grace. For, "the matter that is assigned in the Church of Rome, are the acts of the penitent; his confession by his mouth to the priest, the contrition of his heart, and the satisfaction of his work, in doing the enjoined Penance. The aggregate of all these is the *matter*" of the so-called sacrament; "and the *form* are the words, *I absolve thee.*" Touching the matter, as I said, there is no visible sign applied to the receiver; for thoughts, and words, and actions are not such. And then, as respects the *form*, it is a

Canon ix.

See Burnet on Art. XXV.

See Sessio xiv. c. iii.

[15] I have not given the original Latin, as it would too much encumber the page. It is almost literally translated, and will be found as referred to.

practice of so comparatively recent a
date [16], that it never would have been
hit upon could a better have been devised. In fact, "no ritual can be pro-
duced, nor author cited for this form,
for above a thousand years after Christ;
all the ancient forms of receiving peni-
tents having been a blessing in the form
of a prayer, or a declaration; but none
of them in these positive words, '*I absolve thee* [17].' We think, therefore, this

[16] See what Hooker says: "And albeit Thomas
with his followers have thought it safer to maintain as
well the service of the penitent, as the words of the
minister, necessary unto the essence of this Sacrament;
the services of the penitent as a cause material; the
words of absolution as a formal," &c.—*Eccl. Pol.* vi. c.
iv. § 3.

[17] I may venture to quote here the words of Goar,
from his notes in the Euchologion, "*In Orationes super
Pœnitentes.*" "Atque equidem si ex Ecclesiasticâ
historicâ, ritualibus antiquis, traditione, aut aliis non
excipiendis testimoniis conjicere licet, antiquam in Ecclesiâ Latinâ, Pœnitentiæ Sacramenti sive absolutionis
formam deprecativis verbis compositam fuisse; eamque
indicativam et judicativam ut ita loquar, quâ nunc
utimur, *Absolvo te a peccatis tuis,* quatuor circiter sæcu-
lorum ætatem forsitan non superare," &c.—p. 539,
2nd edit. 1730. Folio.

On the abolishment of Penitentiaries in the Greek

want of *matter*, and this new-invented *form*, being without any institution in Scripture, and different from so long a practice of the whole Church, are such reasons, that we are fully justified in denying Penance to be a sacrament." With the word itself, as synonymous with Repentance, or the worthy fruits of it, we quarrel not,—a sacrament only it is that we deny it to be.

Barnet, ut suprà.

But what is the inference to be drawn from the precepts of the Romish doctrine of Confession, so insisted on there, though doctors of their own Church have felt the unsteadiness of the ground beneath their feet?

Simply, Christian Brethren, this: We are drawn away from the deeply humiliating sense of true repentance, which Christ our Saviour preached as well as His forerunner the Baptist, and all the

Church, and the events that led to it, see Hooker's Eccl. Pol. vi. c. iv. § 9, and on the Introduction of Auricular Confession by Theodore of Tarsus, Abp. of Canterbury, see Johnson's English Canons, p. 87, new edit.

Prophets,—to a hollow, insidious, delusive, and treacherous device of men. For, whenever the Romish Church speaks of Penance, Confession, Absolution, Contrition, Attrition, Satisfaction, or Indulgences,—of which she hath spoken little since Tetzel's [18] rascalities and the days of Luther,—it is the power of the Church, and the power of the priesthood that is uppermost in her thoughts; not the unfathomable mercies of God in Christ! This, at least, is *practically* the

[18] It is needless to recount how Indulgences drew on the Reformation. See Bp. Hall's " No Peace with Rome," § xii. " *Concerning Indulgences or Pardons.*" all registered at a price in their penitentiary tax. " Yea, as Ticelius (*i. e.* Tetzel), the Pope's Pardoner, made his brag in Germany, though a man had 'ravished the Mother of God,' yet so soon as the money did but clink in the bottom of the bason, presently the soul flew out of Purgatory." *Bramhall*, vol. i. 181. Time was it indeed for things to mend, for they had come to the worst!

If my memory does not misgive me, the celebrated iron chest in which Tetzel collected the money for Indulgences is at Weimar. Some such words as these run in my head :—

Sobald das Geld im Kisten klingt,
Sobald die Seel' gen Himmel springt !

P 2

case; for, whatever may be the views of
the better instructed, it is not to be
denied that the word and the absolution
of the priest is to the unlettered laity
pretty much in the place of God's word.
In truth, experience teaches us, that the
whole doctrine of Penance in the Romish Church, under which I include
confession generally, is a doctrine of the
utmost danger to the souls of men. A
fallacy is passed upon the ignorant, and
the blind is made to go out of his way,
which is a sad thing, and subject to the

Deut.
xxvii. 18.

Almighty's denunciation. And then for
the wicked and the profane, they, by
this corruption of doctrine, are led on to
scoff at all that is holy, just, and good.
True it is, the good and the holy-minded,
by God's grace, in any Church, will be
good and holy still, looking only to
Christ's atoning blood shed for the remission of sins; but not so the unclean
and the wicked-hearted. They, as is
known well enough in every-day life,
confess to their priests, and take a new

lease to sin on, and thus hit upon a device which worldly priests encourage for gain ; namely, how their sins may be at once remitted and retained. "The priest remits them by absolution, and the penitent retains them by going on still in the commission of them, in hope of obtaining a new absolution as often as occasion shall require." Such, in no overstrained words, has been the practical working of Confession in the Romish Church; and the good and the holy men with whom that Church has abounded have never been able to repress the flagrant evil. It has burnt up in the light of this sun, and in the broad open day, and in the face of heaven !

But, over and above what has been thus far noted, I must call upon you to observe, that whenever the Romish Church speaks of confession, it is of Auricular Confession, or confession in the ear of the priest, that she speaketh. At least, the exception will prove the rule, and she has used it as " a rack of

Tillotson, vol. ix. 3825.

Jewel, i.
186 ; Jer.
Tayl. xi.
41.

Hooker,
Eccl. Pol.
vi. c. iv. 5.

men's consciences[19]," and in furtherance
of her priestly sway. She speaketh of it
as " commanded, yea, commanded in the
nature of a sacrament, and thereby so
necessary that sin without it cannot be
pardoned." The consequence of which
is, that the timid and the fearful are led
into superstitious scruples, and the fear-
less and the unbelieving to a state the
most dangerous, being led to look upon
religion muchwise in the light of a fable.
Of these, however, I speak not now.
Of the meek-hearted, however, and of
such as would follow on to know the
Lord in the Church's appointed way—

[19] " Rack of conscience" was the common term, and,
as Perkins says, " Instead of two keys Popery hath
devised the picklock of shrift." On *Jude*, vol. iii. 503.

Those who wrote upon the subject of Auricular
Confession in earlier days must have felt this point
acutely, or they had not expressed themselves so
strongly. See, for instance, the words of Bp. Hall, in
his " *Serious Dissuasive from Popery*," where he speaks
of it as " a religion that racks the conscience with the
needless torture of a necessary shrift, wherein the
virtue of absolution depends on the fulness of confession," &c. Works, vol. ii. 642. Folio. Practically, I question if there is any change. The ignorant,
certainly, are still in the like case.

of their distress of mind through the prying of the confessional, it must be said, that nothing can be worse. Books there are which I have read, and which any may read, in which such "*circum-* *stances of confession*" are required, as are ruinous in repetition to the confessor and the confessed. To which the Church of Rome would answer at once, "Such are not accredited formularies; but an abuse of a healthful and holy rite." But, *in practice*, the priests love to have it so; and I do not scruple to say, that it has led to consequences most infamous and most flagitious [20]. History and daily life has recorded them, and they are not to

See Brevint's Saul and Samuel at Endor, p. 124. On the Excuses and Palliations of Romanists, when pressed.

---

[20] "I do willingly conceal from chaste eyes and ears what effects have followed this pretended act of devotion in wanton and unstaid confessors." BP. HALL, "*The Old Religion*," c. xiv. § iii. See what Hey says on Art. XXII. § 15, and Art. XXV. § 4. Perhaps it may not be out of place to refer the reader to Chaucer's "FRERE," in the Prologue to the Canterbury Tales, vv. 218—232.

> "Ful swetely herde he confession,
> And plesant was his absolution.
> He was an esy man to give penance,
> Ther as he wiste to han a good pitance," &c.

be wiped out of our remembrance. And let me add, in well-known words, " Certainly, men lived better lives when, by the discipline of the Church, sinners were brought to public stations and penance, than now they do by all the advantages, real or pretended, from Auricular Confession. And let it be considered, that there being some things, which, St. Paul says, are not to be '*so* 1 Cor. v. 1. *much as named*' amongst Christians, it must needs look indecently, that all men and all women should come and make the priest's ears a common sewer to empty all their filthiness; and that which a modest man would blush to hear, he Jer. Tayl. must be used to, and it is the greatest xi. 33. part of his employment to attend to." That such things are, and are common, is, as I said, sufficiently known,—and Ezek. vii. while this is the case, Penance, as a 5. sacrament, is " *an evil, an only evil,*" and Matt. xxiv. the confessional " *an abomination of de-* 15. *solation,*" far worse than the Romish eagles of old which fled to the prey! And thus, without stopping to speak of

Auricular Confession as "a picklock" which hath been used to open the secrets of states and princes, as tending in its abuse to misrule, to sedition, privy conspiracy, and rebellion, as it hath done, "it is not to be marvelled, that so great a difference appeareth between the doctrine of Rome and our's, when we teach repentance. They imply in the name of repentance much more than we do. We stand chiefly upon the true inward conversion of the heart; they more upon works of external show. We teach, above all things, that repentance which is one and the same from the beginning to the world's end; they a sacramental penance of their own devising and shaping. We labour to instruct men in such sort, that every soul which is wounded with sin may learn the way how to cure itself; they, clean contrary, would make all sores incurable, unless the priest have a hand in them [21]."

Bramhall, v. 223.

Hooker, Eccl. Pol. vi. c. vi. § 2.

[21] See also ibid. vi. c. iv. 14, where the points of difference between God's Church and the Romish Church are severally put, and the conclusion, " That these

As regards the component parts of
Penance insisted on by the Romanists,
it is here out of place to dwell, as it
would carry us to too great length.   It
must not however be omitted that, on
this point, as on others, they make a bad
use of terms unobjectionable in themselves.   For instance, when they say
that CONTRITION, with the priest's absolution, is enough to blot out sins and to
procure our pardon, they say too much.
Lament our sinful lives we do, as much
as they who do so most, bruising [22]
thereby our hearts; but "we acknowledge no contrition at all to be meritorious, save that of Christ, whereby He

Perkins'
Reformed
Catholike,
608.

opinions have youth in their countenance; antiquity
knew them not, it never thought nor dreamed of
them."

[22] See our Homily of Repentance, second part,
where Contrition, as we understand it, is named the
first among the four parts of repentance.   "And verily
this inward sorrow and grief, being conceived in the
heart for the heinousness of sin, if it be earnest and unfeigned, is as a sacrifice to God, as the holy prophet
David doth testify, saying, '*A sacrifice to God is a
troubled spirit : a contrite and a broken heart, O Lord,
thou wilt not despise.*'"   The whole of the Homily on
Repentance is much worth the careful perusal.

was broken for our iniquities." They
speak again of an ATTRITION, or an imperfect contrition, which does not necessarily imply a resolution to sin no more,
and is rather a sorrow for the *conse* See South's
quences of sin, than for *sin itself*, as ab- Serm. vol.
v. 105.
horrent to an all-holy God. But, of
such a component part of Penance as
a sacrament we know nothing. Of it
Tradition muttereth something indis-
tinctly, but God's Word saith nothing
whatever. And when they say that this
fear without love, as they explain Attrition, is invested by absolution of the
priest with such forgiveness as really
purges from sin,—they speak they know
not what, neither do we! Moreover,
in their discussions about SATISFACTION,
although in the Council of Trent they
do assert that it detracteth not from the
merits of Christ, yet, *in practice*, the
people are apt to be led astray, and, as
it were, to call in other means and
appliances besides His most precious
blood poured out. And, therefore, although the ancients spake of amend-

ment of life, and the bringing forth
worthy fruits of penance, as a satisfaction, as men speak, we do rather avoid
the word, lest the ignorant and the unwary should bethink them of trafficking
with God, and a setting up of a mere
sorrowing for sin, not as a merchandise [23]
only, but as an Atonement with the
Almighty, before whom Christ crucified
is the one and alone sacrifice and Atonement for the many sins of this naughty
world. And I speak not, Christian
Brethren, of merchandise and trafficking
in holy things without a cause; for
closely connected with the sacrament of
Penance is the Romanist figment of
Purgatory [24],——to which, in this sense,

---

[23] See Burnet on Art. XXV. and Jewel's Defence
of the Apology, part v., who tells Harding, that " of
the shameless merchandize and sales hereof many
godly men have complained." Vol. vi. 129. To which
may be added Stavely's " Roman Horseleech," c. vii.,
Indulgences, Pardons, &c., p. 46, &c.

[24] It may be noted here, that the Council of Trent
defines nothing. See *Sessio* xxx. The " Catechismus" does. See " De Symbolo Fidei," Art. v., " Pur-
gatorius ignis," &c.

St. Augustine [25] gives no encourage-
ment,—and their doctrine of Pardons or
Indulgences. And to the point spake
he who said, that " at this postern gate
cometh in the whole mart of Papal indulgences, so infinitely strewed, that the
pardon of sin, which heretofore was obtained hardly and by much suit, is with
them become now almost impossible to
be escaped."

Hooker,
Eccl. Pol.
vi. c. vi. § 7.
and suprà,
vi. c. v. § 9.

And thus, in due course, have I
opened to you the question of Romish
Penance, and its concomitant circumstances ; and it was necessary so to do,

---

[25] On this point, see Jewel's Defence of the Apology, &c., part ii. After quoting the several passages
relative to the question, he thus sums up : " By
these it is plain, that St. Augustine stood in doubt
hereof, whether there be any such *purgatory fire*, or
no. Therefore, undoubtedly, he looked at neither for
an *article of the Christian faith* (for thereof it has not
been lawful for him to doubt), nor for any *tradition of
the Apostles*." Vol. v. 209. See also Hey on Art.
XXII. § 2, and a striking passage in Jewel, vol. vii.
170. But we may repeat his after words, " But where
now is purgatory? who regardeth it? who careth for
it? Children scorn it in their streets, and know it is
a fable. How cometh this so to pass? The wicked
or lawless man is revealed." *Ibid.* p. 183.

because by it the priest is made a certain sort of intercessor for sinners; whereas the Scripture teacheth us that Christ is our alone Intercessor, in this sense,—that He alone receiveth and offereth up the prayers of penitent souls,— that He alone, " by one most precious and propitiatory sacrifice, which was His body, a gift of infinite worth, offered for the sins of the whole world, hath thereby once reconciled us to God, purchased His general free pardon, and turned away divine indignation from mankind."

Hooker, ut suprà, vi. c. v. § 3.

It remains but to say that we, who have been redeemed by His all-precious blood which cleanseth us from all sin, must not run into the contrary extreme, and so reject the ministry of reconciliation; for it is a very different thing blindly to submit to priestcraft, and heedlessly to spurn at those apostles, prophets, evangelists, pastors and teachers, into whose keeping, ordinarily, Christ hath committed the sacred deposit of His Holy Sacraments, and unto whom He hath given power, ministerially, to proclaim the forgiveness of those sins on earth (*when humbly and heartily desired* [26]), which are already forgiven in heaven! Such a dispensation of comforting mercy forget we not, for it is a heavenly gift! yea, given "*for the perfecting of the saints, for the work of the ministry, for the edifying of the body of Christ. Till we all come in the unity of the faith, and of the knowledge of the Son of God, unto a perfect man, unto the measure of the stature of the fulness of Christ.*" *Ephes. iv. 12, 13.*

Can I conclude better than in holy David's words? "THOU *hast forgiven the offence of Thy people, and covered all their sins.* THOU *hast taken away all Thy displeasure, and turned Thyself from Thy wrathful indignation.* TURN US THEN, O GOD OUR SAVIOUR, AND LET THINE ANGER CEASE FROM US!" *Ps. lxxxv 2 – 4.*

---

[26] See Rubric before Absolution in the "*Visitation of the Sick.*" Individually, I can conceive no greater comfort than the blessing of a holy man, in God's name! Who can ever forget a father's or a mother's blessing? I should pity such.

SERMON VI.

PART I.

THE FAITH ONCE DELIVERED UNTO THE SAINTS.

Q

"Credite experto, quasi Christianus Christianis loquor. Venenata sunt illius dogmata, aliena à Scripturis Sanctis, vim Scripturis facientia."—HIEROM. *ad Pammac. et Ocean.* tom. i. 521. A.

"Quisquis es assertor novorum dogmatum, quæso te, ut parcas Romanis auribus ; parcas fidei, quæ Apostoli voce laudata est. Cur post quadringentos annos docere nos niteris, quod ante nescivimus ! cur profers in medium, quod Petrus et Paulus edere noluerunt ! Usque ad hunc diem sine istâ doctrinâ mundus Christianus fuit. Illam senex tenebo fidem, in quâ puer renatus sum."—IBID. p. 526. E.

Τὸ δὲ πᾶν διὰ τὸν Θεὸν πράττομεν, καὶ ὥστε ἐκεῖνον περὶ δογμάτων ἀπολογήσασθαι τούτων· ὁ μὲν γὰρ ἀνθρώπους θέλων πεῖσαι πολλὰ ὕπουλα ποιεῖ, καὶ διεστραμμένα, καὶ ἀπάτῃ κέχρηται καὶ ψεύδει, ὥστε πεῖσαι καὶ ἑλεῖν τὴν τῶν ἀκουόντων γνώμην· ὁ δὲ Θεὸν πείθων, καὶ ἀρέσκειν ἐκείνῳ σπουδάζων, ἁπλῆς δεῖται διανοίας καὶ καθαρᾶς· ἀνεξαπάτητον γὰρ τὸ θεῖον· ὅθεν δῆλον ὅτι καὶ ἡμεῖς, φησιν, οὐ φιλαρχίας ἕνεκεν, οὐδὲ ὥστε μαθητὰς ἔχειν, οὐδὲ τῆς παρ' ὑμῶν ἐφιέμενοι δόξης ταῦτα γράφομεν· οὐ γὰρ ἀνθρώποις ἀρέσαι ἐσπουδάκαμεν, ἀλλὰ Θεῷ.— CHRYSOST. *in c. i. Epist. ad Galat. Comment.* tom. x. 671. D.

Καὶ τί λέγω; οὐδὲ Παύλῳ πείθεσθαι χρή, ἄν τι ἴδιον λέγῃ, ἄν τι ἀνθρώπινον, ἀλλὰ τῷ Ἀποστόλῳ τῷ τὸν Χριστὸν ἔχοντι λαλοῦντα ἐν ἑαυτῷ.—IBID. *in 2 Epist. ad Timoth. c. i. Hom.* ii. tom. xi. 669. E.

Μαχαίρας δίκην τέμνε τὰ περισσὰ καὶ νοθὰ δόγματα, ἃ οἱ ἀπολλύμενοι προσετρέψαντο τῷ κηρύγματι, καὶ εἰς τὸ εὐθὲς ἄγε διὰ τοῦ Πνεύματος.—ŒCUMEN. *Com. in 2 Tim.* ii. 15. tom. ii. 247.

Εἰ φιλομαθῶς ἐζήτεις τὰς γραφὰς, εὕρισκες δὲ ἑτέρας ἐκεῖθεν μαρτυρίας, διασαφούσας σοι τὸ κινούμενον.— ISIDOR. *Pelusiot.* lib. i. 449. p. 114.

"Propositum mihi erat, non ad meam voluntatem Scripturas trahere, sed id dicere, quod Scripturas velle intelligebam. Commentatoris officium est non quod ipse velit : sed quid sentiat ille, quem interpretatur, exponere. Alioqui si contraria dixerit, non tam interpres erit, quam adversarius ejus, quem nititur explanare."—HIEROM. *Epist.* xlviii. *ad Pammach.* tom. i. 227. E.

"Omne quod non ædificat audientes, in periculum vertitur loquentium. Ego si fecero, si dixero quippiam, quod reprehensione dignum est : de sanctis egredior, et polluo vocabulum Christi, in quo mihi blandior."—IBID. *Epist.* lxiv. *ad Fabiolam.* tom. i. 356. B.

SERMON VI.

PART I.

THE FAITH ONCE DELIVERED UNTO THE SAINTS.

JUDE ver. 3.

" Beloved, when I gave all diligence to write unto you of the common salvation, it was needful for me to write unto you, and exhort you that ye should earnestly contend for the faith which was once delivered unto the Saints."

THESE words of St. Jude, Christian Brethren, are fitting ones for the matter we yet have in hand, which is, to complete our survey of Romish errors. For one or two points have still to be referred to, although hinted at, and even mentioned, in what has previously been said. The words, moreover, of *" Jude,*

Q 2

the servant of Jesus Christ, and brother of James, to them that are sanctified by God the Father, and preserved in Jesus Christ and called,"—words wherein the

ver. 1, 2.

increase of "*mercy, and peace, and love,*" is heartily wished for,—are good words and comfortable words for us all, containing as they do an earnest exhortation to individuals,—to you, and me, and all of us,—to abide in our Christian calling.   And, not only so, but to maintain, at all hazards, THE TRUTH AS IT IS

Ephes. iv. 21.

IN JESUS, which truth ye have heard, and in which ye have been taught and catechised from your childhood to this day, "*looking,*" I trust, "*for that blessed hope, and the glorious appearing of the great God and our Saviour Jesus Christ, Who gave Himself for us, that He might redeem us from all iniquity, and purify unto Himself a peculiar people, zealous of*

Tit. ii. 13, 14.

good works."   For this is "*the common*

Tit. i. 4.

faith," this is the "*common salvation!*" and such as receive it rightly, and lay it up in their heart of hearts, and show it forth in their daily conversation, acknow-

ledge " *the truth which is after godliness.*" Tit. i. 1.
And although, under ordinary circum-
stances, "*the servant of the Lord must
not strive*" in the world's strife, "*but be
gentle unto all men, apt to teach, patient,
In meekness instructing those that oppose
themselves ; if God peradventure will give
them repentance to the acknowledging of
the truth ; And that they may recover
themselves out of the snare of the devil,* 2 Tim. ii.
who are taken captive by him at his will;" 24—26.
yet, against innovations on the faith he
must set his face like a flint.   Ay,
Christian Brethren, one and all of us,
however little we like to move out of
our quiet sphere, must "*stand fast in one
spirit, with one mind, striving together
for the faith of the Gospel ;*"—"*war* " we Phil. i. 27.
must a "*good warfare, holding faith and* 1 Tim. i.
a good conscience," if so be we may "*lay* 18, 19.
hold on eternal life, whereunto " we are 1 Tim. vi.
"*also called,*" like as were those whom 12.
Jude exhorted in the text that they
should "*earnestly contend for the faith
which was once delivered unto the saints ;*"
that is to say, once for all delivered to
the Apostles of our Lord and Saviour

Jesus Christ, and by them [1] to such as were called to the knowledge of the truth, without alterations and without additions.   And hence St. Paul spoke in such strong terms to the Galatian converts, "*Though we, or an angel from heaven, preach any other Gospel unto you than that which we have preached unto you, let him be accursed.   As we said before, so say I now again, If any man preach any other Gospel unto you than that ye have received, let him be accursed ;*" bear that curse [2] which all must bear who pervert the Gospel of Christ, and repent

Gal. i. 8, 9.

---

[1] " Eam dicit *semel traditam sanctis* Fidem,—id est, iis qui nunc sancti sunt, nempe per Apostolos, ut 1 Cor. xi. 2. 23 ; xv. 3."—GROTIUS in loc.

[2] In the first instance this no doubt referred to excommunication.   See Hammond's note on Rom. ix. 3. SCHOETTGEN's words on Gal. i. 8 are remarkable : " Quibus sane verbis saniores quoque Judæi ostendunt, ultrà verbum revelatum nihil esse adsumendum, quamvis etiam revelatione extraordinariâ cœlesti manifestarentur." Tom. i. 727.   He evidently was thinking upon the tradition of the Romanists.   I need hardly say that this text precludes all modern notions of DEVELOPMENT,—if modern they are to be called.   Of this sort is the still pending question of the " Immaculate Conception" of the Virgin Mary.   I need scarcely refer my readers to the Encyclic Letter of the present Pope, dated Cajeta, February 2, 1849.

not of the evil they have done. Hence too that painful summing-up of the Scripture of Truth in the Revelation of St. John the Divine, "*I testify unto every man that heareth the words of the prophecy of this book, If any man shall add unto these things, God shall add unto him the plagues that are written in this book. And if any man shall take away from the words of the book of this prophecy, God shall take away his part out of the book of life, and out of the holy city, and from the things which are written in this book.*" Of such consequence is it, Christian Brethren, that "*ye should earnestly contend for the faith once delivered unto the saints !* " Rev. xxii. 18, 19.

Now, those who had perverted "*the simplicity that is in Christ,*" as we see from these words of Jude, had already arisen,—heretics of that day, whom it is not necessary to speak of here [3]. St. 2 Cor. xi. 3.

---

[3] Theophylact's words are : Λέγει δὲ τοὺς ἀπὸ Νικολάου, καὶ Οὐαλεντίνου, καὶ Σίμωνος τῶν μιαρωτάτων. Tom. iii. 447. B. And to the same purpose Œcumenius in loc., tom. ii. 623. B. I may refer here to an excellent Sermon of Hickes' on this text, in which

Peter also spake of like false teachers, who "*privily*" should "*bring in damnable heresies.*" St. Paul too had said to the Corinthians, "*There must be also heresies among you, that they which are approved may be made manifest among you.*" And, one greater than Jude, or Peter, or Paul, even their Lord and Master, as well as ours, hath told us what we are to expect in the field of this world. "*Good seed*" hath he sown there,—but an enemy hath come and sowed tares among the wheat, and "*the enemy that sowed them is the devil.*" In the world he found a fitting soil,—even man's corrupt heart [4], and there, with

2 Pet. ii. 1.

1 Cor. xi. 19.

Matt. xiii. 39.

he points out clearly and from antiquity how the Romanists have corrupted the faith. Vol. ii. 213, &c. 8vo. 1713.

[4] See Abp. Whately on the Origin of Romish Errors. " The Romish system rose insensibly like a young plant from the seed, making a progress scarcely perceptible from year to year, till at length it had fixed its root deeply in the soil, and spread its baneful shade far around.

Infæcunda quidem, sed læta et fortia surgunt,
Quippe solo natura subest ;

it was the natural offspring of man's frail and corrupt

all deceivableness, he sought to implant such erroneous doctrines as should lead to utter destruction and misery.

And thus it was, as with other corruptions, so with those of the Papacy. Man, being evil, out of an evil heart of mistrust and unbelief, did not "*follow on to know the Lord*," as the Lord had taught him, whether by His Prophets of old, or by the Scriptures of His truth [5]. On the contrary, he hit upon devices of his own, as though the revelation of God's will were imperfect; and when he followed the desires of his own heart they led him astray, for that "*the heart is deceitful above all things, and despe-*

Hos. vi. 3.

character, and it needed no sedulous culture." c. i. p. 11. *Superstition.*

[5] "It is a free challenge betwixt us, let the elder have us both : if there be any point of our religion younger than the Patriarchs, and Prophets, and CHRIST, and His Apostles, the Fathers and the Doctors of the Primitive Church, let it be accursed and condemned for an upstart : show us evidence of more credit and age, and carry it. The Church of Rome hath been ancient, not the errors ; neither do we in ought differ from it, wherein it is not departed from itself."—BP. HALL, "*Serious Dissuasive from Popery,*" vol. i. 634.

rately wicked." Err and wander from the right way all men have done and will do, Protestants as well as Papists, one with another, when once they let go God's holy Word, which is committed to their trust, and is "*a lantern unto their feet, and a light unto their paths.*" The revelation of His will once granted, as it is granted in the pages of the New Testament once for all, we have no alternative, as we would be saved, but to follow it. For that men did not so, the dimness of their vexation came upon them; and that great darkness which brooded for so long a time upon the nations was the sure and natural result. A time, possibly, not of so great darkness as some have thought [6]; but dark and dreary, nevertheless, because "*Christ and Him crucified*" was not uppermost

Jer. xxii. 9.

Ps. cxix. 105.

1 Cor. ii. 2.

[6] I beg to refer the curious reader to Maitland's "Dark Ages;" and he should read the Preface to that curious work, that the writer's views may not be mistaken. I may likewise refer also to his other volume connected with the subject before me—"Essays on Subjects connected with the Reformation in England."

in men's minds, and therefore trouble was right at hand.

And in these days of darkness was it that the corruption of the human heart, coupled with its superstitions and its fears, led on to the corruptions of the Papacy. Ignorant were the bulk of the people, and easily deceived,—corrupt also were many of the priesthood, and ready to deceive them. And, without entering upon a matter of long discussion, a vast superstructure was, by degrees, erected upon "*stones of emptiness*,"—upon "*wood, hay, and stubble*,"—whereas, to withstand the wear and tear of this world, and to abide for a better, "*other foundation can no man lay than that is laid, which is Jesus Christ.*" In His own all-sacred words, "*Whosoever heareth these sayings of Mine, and doeth them, I will liken him unto a wise man, which built his house upon a rock. And the rain descended, and the floods came, and the winds blew, and beat upon that house; and it fell not, for it was founded upon a rock. And every one that heareth*

Isa. xxxiv. 11.

1 Cor. iii. 12.

1 Cor. iii. 11.

*these sayings of Mine and doeth them not,
shall be likened unto a foolish man, which
built his house upon the sand.   And the
rain descended, and the floods came, and*

Matt. vii.
24—27.

*the winds blew, and beat upon that house ;
and it fell, and great was the fall of it* [7]*."*
And so, Christian Brethren, will all
those churches and individuals fall who
rest not in Christ ; for God *" hath put
all things under His feet, and gave Him
to be the head over all things to the*

Ephes. i.
22, 23.

*Church, which is His body, the fulness of
Him that filleth all in all."*   Even so.
He is not the FOUNDATION only, and the
CHIEF CORNER-STONE,—but the HEAD
likewise !   Without Him we can do
nothing towards spiritual edification !
As many as are built up in a Faith
most holy are His building.   To this
end the Comforter came, and speaketh
to us still, and completes the building
up of Christian men.   To this end He
said, Who spake not as man speaks, *" The
Comforter, which is the Holy Ghost,*

[7] See South's striking Sermon on this text, vol. ii.
324, &c.

whom the Father will send in My name,
He shall teach you all things, and bring
all things to your remembrance, whatso-   John xiv.
ever I have said unto you."   Such is our 26.
true state.   The evil that is in us is our   Ezek. xiii.
own *"untempered morter,"*—any good 10.
we have is wrought of God!   In those
words of St. Paul to his Ephesian converts, *"By grace are ye saved through*
faith, and not that of yourselves; it is
the gift of God: not of works, lest any
man should boast. For we are His work-
manship, created in Christ Jesus unto
good works, which God hath before or-   Ephes. ii.
dained that we should walk in them."   8—10.

Which things if ye will consider,
Christian Brethren, ye will readily conclude how all our own corruptions are
opposed to Christ, and how fatal those
corruptions of the Romish Church are
which lead away our thoughts from God
and from His Christ.   And therefore
was it necessary to dwell upon the
Scriptures alone, apart from all Traditions, written or unwritten, as in them
is contained all that concerns us to

know touching our everlasting salvation.
Therefore was it necessary to dwell
upon the Church of God, showing it to
be founded on the Scriptures and subject to Christ, THE HEAD,—and not so
to speak of it as lightly [8] to apprehend
Christ, " *Who loved the Church, and gave
Himself for it.*" Therefore was it necessary to dwell upon the "*one Mediator
between God and men, the man Christ
Jesus, Who gave Himself a ransom for
all;*" because, in course of time, foolish
men had introduced other means of
drawing nigh unto God than Himself
had appointed, such as the Virgin Mother, and the Intercession of Saints, and

Ephes. v.
25.

1 Tim. ii.
5, 6.

---

[8] Perkins says, on Jude ver. 8, " I believe not, because the Church saith so, but because the Scripture
saith it ; and the Church I believe so far as she con-
sents with the Word, and speaketh out of it." Vol. iii.
492.   In treating on this verse of Jude he touches
severally on Roman Catholic and other errors.   Of
our own desertion of the faith so often, in our lives,
he says pointedly : " Yea, our common Protestants,
who in judgment acknowledge this rite, yet in their
life they leave it, and take the leaden rule of natural
reason, sense, sight, and feeling ; and few there be that
live by faith." Ibid. p. 493.

other devices, I know not what or how
many. Therefore was it necessary to
speak to you of those Sacraments which
Christ ordained as generally necessary
to salvation,—for that the Romanists
had introduced others, and had forced
them on the consciences of men, under
the penalty of being accursed of God,—
to say nothing of that high idolatry in
Transubstantiation, and the gross wickedness of depriving the people of the cup,
touching which Christ Himself did say,
"DRINK YE ALL OF IT;" by the which
robbery, as it might be called, but that
God can work with or without means,
we know not what hurt might have
been done to the souls of men. Then,
again, was it necessary to dwell upon
the Romish interpretation of Penance,
which they had turned into a sacrament,—thereby to magnify the power
of priestcraft, as we may rightly
denominate the corruption of a holy
and delegated office, under Christ,—
by tampering with Pardons or Indulgences and the Fire of Purgatory, in the

stead of dealing holily and wisely with the sacred rites of Confession and Absolution, wherewith to ease men's consciences, and to comfort those, in Christ's name, who grieved for their sins, and were heartily sorry for their offences!

These, and other like points, Christian Brethren, was it necessary to dwell upon, and to disabuse your minds also of what the Romanists call the Catholic Church,——thereby meaning their own Church only, which has grown to be what it is by the corrupt following of the Apostles, and other their idle but subtle insinuations of Infallibility and Supremacy [9]. Moreover, you do well to bear in mind, that by this their sort of speech you are excluded, as heretics, from the pale of salvation. For, when the Romanists say that without the Church there is no salvation, the Church they mean is their own.

[9] To claim universality as if by the institution of Christ, is to make herself, says Abp. Bramhall, "the mother of her grandmother, the Church of Jerusalem, and the mistress of her many elder sisters." Vol. i. 26.

But, blessed be God! His Holy Church standeth not in what men say, but in His mercy, which endureth for ever,— and Him to serve, as ye may serve Him, in a Church so purely reformed, in theory, as the one to which you are privileged to belong *"is good and accept-able in the sight of God our Saviour, Who will have all men to be saved, and to come to the knowledge of the truth."* Such is His wish, and to all who reject not His words giveth He the power. Grace and heavenly benediction He poureth down upon the willing-hearted as the dew of heaven,—and for the ministry, He sendeth them not forth to ban and curse with bell, book, and candle; but both by their life and doc-trine to set forth His glory, and to set forward the salvation of all men, through and by His holy name [10]. Such is His goodness, such is His mercy towards us!

1 Tim. ii. 3, 4.
θέλει.

See 1st Prayer for the Ember Weeks.

[10] Isidore of Pelusium's words are a good motto for any earnest minister of the Gospel : Τούτου μόνου ἐκθύμως περιέχομαι, τοῦ βούλεσθαι πάντας, τόγε ἡμέ-τερον μέρος, σωθῆναι. Lib. iii. Epist. 366. p. 899. D. ed. 1638.

R

But, passing over our own errors of
life and practice, which, more or less,
are Sunday after Sunday laid before
you,—reminding you at the same time
that all the errors of the Romanist proceed from the same source,—that is to
say, the corruption of the human heart,—
I must hasten to call your attention to
a point or two not to be omitted, or ever
I conclude.

And first, to say nothing of the somewhat more intricate point of Free-Will[11],
and referring you for that point to the
words of our tenth Article, wherein,
contrary to the Canons of Trent, we
assert that *unassisted* man cannot do
works pleasant and acceptable to God,—
I would the rather insist upon the Ro-

[11] On points of difference the reader may see Bp.
HALL's "*No Peace with Rome*," § viii. vol. i. 665,
folio ; PERKINS' *Reformed Catholike*, § i.   "The
Papists say, man's will concurreth and worketh with
God's graces in the first conversion of a sinner, *by
itself*, and by its own natural power ; and is only
helped by the Holy Ghost.   We say, that man's will
worketh with grace in the first conversion ; yet not
of itself, but by grace," &c. &c.   Vol. i. 552.

manist corruption of, what they call, Inherent Righteousness. And this I would
do because the best of us, at all times,
are for thinking better of ourselves than
we ought to think; whereas, at best, we
are poor miserable sinners, and that
saying of the prophet is only true,
"THEIR RIGHTEOUSNESS IS OF ME, SAITH
THE LORD!" But what saith the Church Isa. liv. 17.
of Rome? "If any one shall say that
by *faith alone* the wicked is justified,
understanding thereby that *nothing else*
is required, by way of co-operation, in
attaining the grace of Justification; and
that in nowise is it necessary that a man
be prepared and set in order by *the
motion of his own will ;*—let him be ac- Sess. vi.
cursed." Directly contrary to which is Canon ix.
the teaching of Scripture. There we
are instructed in this truth, that inherent righteousness is not in man. The
faith that justifies is of Christ alone [12],—

---

[12] See Perkins' "Exposition upon the Epistle of
Jude :" I. What it is to be justified. II. What it is to
be justified by faith. III. What works are to be excluded from justification. Vol. iii. 499. Add to this

and in that we live, we live by Him. As St. Paul said to the Galatians, " *The life which I now live in the flesh, I live* Gal. ii. 20. *by the faith of the Son of God.*" To the Philippians : *Yea, doubtless, and I count all things but loss, for the excellency of the knowledge of Christ Jesus, my Lord ; for whom I have suffered the loss of all things, and do count them but dung that I may win Christ, and be found in Him, not having mine own righteousness, which is of the law, but that which is through the faith of Christ, the righteousness which* Phil. iii. *is of God by faith.*" So speaketh Scrip- 8, 9. ture, so speaketh the Romish Church by that Council which prescribed her formularies. The one pointeth to Christ alone, the other to some " divine quality inherent," which, as far as we can find, " *the wickedness*" of whose " *heels* " com- passeth us about, is not within the coil of this mortal flesh. Indeed, indeed, ye Christian People, it is simply thus:

the words of Cassander and Thomas Aquinas, referred to by Bp. Hall, " No Peace with Rome," § vii. vol. i. p. 663.

"Christ hath merited righteousness for as many as are found in Him. In Him God findeth us, if we be faithful; for by faith we are incorporated into Him. Then, although in ourselves we be altogether sinful and unrighteous, yet even the man which in himself is impious, full of iniquity, full of sin; him being found in Christ through faith, and having his sin in hatred through repentance; him God beholdeth with a gracious eye, putteth away his sin by not imputing it, taketh quite away the punishment due thereto, by pardoning it; and accepteth him in Jesus Christ, as perfectly righteous, as if he had fulfilled all that is commanded him in the law; shall, I say, be more perfectly righteous than if himself had fulfilled the whole law. I must take heed what I say; but the Apostle saith, *'God made Him, which knew no sin, to be sin for us; that we might be made the righteousness of God in Him.'* Such we are in the sight of 2 Cor. 21. God the Father, as is the very Son of God Himself. Let it be counted folly,

or phrensy, or fury, or whatsoever, it is
our comfort, and our wisdom.   We care
for no knowledge in the world but this,
that man hath sinned, and God hath

HOOKER,
on Justifi-
cation,
Serm. ii.
§ 6.

suffered ; that God hath made Himself
the sin of man, and that men are made
the righteousness of God."   So far are
we from speaking of Inherent Righteousness of Justification !   Yea, rather,
we do simply confess, " *Take away his*

Ps. x. 17.

Rom. iii.
10. ; Ps.
xiv. 4.

ungodliness, and thou shalt find none,"—
not a man !   " *There is none righteous,
no, not one !* "   And, without speaking
of Righteousness of Justification and
Righteousness of Sanctification, which
may be distinguished, we say rather, in
the words of our Article, " We are accounted righteous before God only for
the merit of our Lord and Saviour Jesus
Christ, by faith, and not for our own

Art. XI.

works or deservings."   Pass we over
also all discussion relative to the distinction between a *justifying* Faith and a
lively Faith [13], as turning upon the same

---

[13] Bp. MARSH observes, " It is a *mistake* that, according to the tenets of our Church, *justifying* faith is

point,—for truer words than these were never spoken: "It must be only under the garment of our Elder Brother, that we dare come in for a blessing. His righteousness, made ours by Faith, is that whereby we are justified in the sight of God."

Bp. HALL, " The Old Religion," c. v. § 1.

II. Yet, again, Christian Brethren, be on your guard against any such teaching as shall cause you to make such a distinction between *mortal* and *venial* sin,

a *lively* faith. According to the tenets of our Church, it neither *is*, nor *can be*, such. And it is the want of *distinction* between *justifying* faith and *lively* faith, to which we may entirely ascribe the numerous inconsistencies and contradictions in which the doctrine of justification has, within these few years, been involved. When our twelfth Article asserts, that 'a *lively* faith may be as evidently known as a tree is discerned by the *fruit*,' the Article alludes to works, which, as there stated, 'follow *after* justification.' Indeed the thirteenth Article denies even the *possibility* of good works *before* justification. The faith, therefore, which had *previously justified*, cannot have been a *lively* or *productive* faith. For then it would have been a faith accompanied with good works, which, *before* justification, cannot even *exist*. The doctrine of justification therefore, as maintained by the Church of *England*, is decidedly at variance with the doctrine of the Church of Rome." *Comparative View*, c. iii. p. 51.

as do the Romanists,—for this, *in practice*, leads to the depreciation of Christ's Atonement, and the oneness of His Mediatorship, suggesting the idea, that "some sins, though offences against God, and violations of His law, can be of their own nature such slight things, that they deserve only temporal punishment, and may be expiated by some piece of penance or devotion, or the communication of the merits of others." Certainly God's Holy Word admits of no such distinction.   And who, and be guiltless, "*hath despised the day of small things?*"   The truth is, that every sin, when looked upon as a little one, at once becomes great in the sight of God! The very thought is presumption; and true as the truest are the words of the Psalmist, "*Who can tell how oft he offendeth?   O cleanse thou me from my secret faults.   Keep Thy servant also from presumptuous sins, lest they get the dominion over me; so shall I be undefiled, and innocent from the great offence.*" The lack of this humble-mindedness led to

Burnet, on Art. XVI.

Zech. iv. 10.

Ps. xix. 12, 13.

the distinction here alluded to, which
still runs in the groove of that great
imposture—Romish Infallibility and Supremacy! The merits of the saints were
laid up, as it were, in a treasure-house,
or in a bank of faith, and the surplusage
ran into a common stock [14], to be doled
out by virtue of Papal Indulgences;
as though man, "*that is a worm*," and Job xxv.6.
"*a sinner from the womb*," could be just Isa. xlviii. 8.
in the sight of an all-holy God, and help
himself, much less lay up merits for
another, and make agreement for the
pardon of transgression! No wonder,
Christian Brethren, that such teaching
as this, carried to extremes, led on to
the Reformation! No wonder that it
was clearly set forth in our Articles
that "voluntary works besides, over and
above, God's commandments, which they
call works of supererogation [15]," cannot

[14] These words are Hooker's, slightly altered. He
is speaking of the ground of Satisfaction by the Pope's
Indulgence. See Eccl. Pol. Book vi. c. v. § 9.

[15] The following extract is from Hey. It is long,
but to the point; and was not so easily worked up
into the context: " The Council of Trent seems to

be taught without arrogancy and impiety; for by them men do declare that

avoid the term supererogation, though it calls *Indulgences* ' cœlestes Ecclesiæ *Thesauros.*' This conduct favours the idea, that the Romish Church rather wishes to have the doctrine of Supererogation believed by the *people*, than precisely *taught* to all men of improved minds.   The Rhemish Testament, which was intended for those who understood English and not Latin, speaks plainly (on 2 Cor. viii. 14), ' Holy Sainctes, or other vertuous persons, may in measure and proportion of other men's necessities and deservings, allotte unto them, as well the *Supererogation* of their spiritual workes, as those that abound in worldly goods, may give alone of their superfluities to them which are in necessitie.'   The *Necessary Doctrine* seems to have adopted *reformed* notions in this particular; for here Reformation began; it uses the *text* (Luke xvii. 10) which is in our Article, and exhorts men to keep continually advancing in virtue; and represents them, the farther they advance, as being the more *indebted* to God for His Grace, which enabled them to advance.   It also represents our duties as being enjoined, not for any benefit to God, but merely for our *own good*.   The third part of our *Homily* on Good Works, turns to ridicule the *Lamps* always running over, the markets of merits, the works of overflowing abundance, of Supererogatory Papists; and by so doing, shows how necessary it was, at the time of the Reformation, to expose the corrupt practices and superstitions of the Romish Church, to the *people;* and to declare against such corruptions in the new body of doctrines." Book iv. Art. xiv. § 2.

they do not only render unto God as much as they are bound to do, but that they do more for His sake than of bounden duty is required: whereas, Christ saith plainly, " *When you have done all that is commanded to you,* Luke xvii. *say, We are unprofitable servants.*" As 10 ; Art. XIV. it is expressed in the Article that follows, It is Christ alone that is without sin! "But all we the rest, although baptized and born again in Christ, yet offend in many things; and *if we say we have no sin, we deceive ourselves, and the truth is not in us.*" So wisely, 1 John i. 8 so cautiously in Scripture words, spake Art. XV. our Reformers! So thoughtfully, and with humbleness of mind, spake he who said, "The best things we do have somewhat in them to be pardoned. How then can we do any thing meritorious, and worthy to be rewarded? Indeed, God doth liberally promise whatsoever appertaineth to a blessed life, unto as many as sincerely keep His law, though they be not able exactly to keep it. Wherefore, we acknowledge a dutiful necessity of doing well; but the meritorious dignity of well-doing we utterly renounce. We see how far we are from the perfect righteousness of the law. The little fruit which we have in holiness, it is, God knoweth, corrupt and unsound: we put no confidence at all in it, we challenge nothing in the world for it. We dare not call God to a reckoning, as if we had Him in our debt-books: our continual suit to Him is and must be, to bear with our infirmities, to pardon our offences!"

HOOKER, on Justification, Serm. ii. § 7.

But time warns me to bring these remarks to a close, and I shall therefore pass by many other points [16] in which,

[16] I may here mention that the very general use of Translations has made it *not altogether needless*, but *less needful*, to dwell upon the subject of our XXIVth Article : " *Of speaking in the Congregation in such a tongue as the People understandeth.*" To speak also of the Celibacy of the Clergy, and of Vows, and of Monastic Institutions, did not fall within the scope of these Discourses. St. Chrysostom's words are applicable here : Τὸ μὴ πάντα περιεργάζεσθαι, καὶ τὸ μὴ πάντα θέλειν εἰδέναι, μέγα τοῦ εἰδέναι τεκμήριον. Hom. viii. in 2 Tim. iii. 14. Tom. xi. 711. I am quite aware that these remarks have already run out too long.

as we would "*earnestly contend for the Faith which was once delivered unto the Saints,*" we cannot join hands with the Romanists, who seek not only for spiritual, but for temporal domination also! Not only would they enslave your consciences, Christian Brethren, but your persons also! For, constituted as the Romish Church is, otherwise she cannot do! Pledged is she to the course she pursues, and she must and will pursue it unto the end! But if so, what peace can there be in her borders, when her "*whoredoms and her witchcrafts are so many?*" When she would lead our 2 Kings people so far astray, not only from their proper Sovereign, but from the King of kings, THE LORD OUR RIGHTEOUSNESS! Alas! The way of peace she hath not known, but has persecuted us to the uttermost since the day we broke off from her corruptions! Ay, because we fall not in with the additions even she has made to the Creed, she proclaims us HERETICS, severed from the Holy Catholic Church of Christ! As in days gone by, so in the present day too, her so-called and usurped Supremacy is but stirring up strife all the day long! She may seem to sleep awhile, but she sleepeth not at all,—yea, rather, is wide awake and on her watch behind her scarlet throne! Let any look into the question that have the means and the power,—let any examine the history of the Church of Rome, from first to last, and they shall find that, in one way or another—I stop not to inquire if of late by their emissaries the Jesuits, or by Dispensations, or by other subtle and unholy sleights—she has made the breaches in the Church she has the effrontery to complain of! This, Christian Brethren, I believe to be as near the truth as may be; and if so,—having granted unto them, as a body, all political concessions [17], and having removed

[17] Without in any ways conceding the wisdom of the measure of 1829, I very willingly now quote the words of Lord Stanley : "I should be the last man to consent to the introduction of any measure which would deprive any portion of my countrymen of the free and full exercise of their religious opinions, and

all such restrictions as could be justly
complained of,—let us now look to ourselves; first, to the doctrine of our
Church which they would undermine;
secondly, to our constitution which they
would pull down about our ears. In
any further concessions, let us look well
and warily to results. Let us not put
our own Church and people into their
power [18], which is what they anticipate,
and what they will be behindhand in
no casuistry to compass. Witness their
power over great minds perverted, and
of whose holiness it would be a sin to
doubt! Witness their deceit in giving to
dishonesty a specious face, and in putting
wrong in the place of right, where the
interests of a corrupt Church are at
stake. "Be as moderate as you please

the free and full performance of their religious duties.
But I must draw a distinction between penal laws
directed against religious opinions, and Parliamentary
legislation directed against foreign usurpation."—THE
TIMES, *March* 1st, 1851.

[18] What a plain countryman said to me but a day
or two ago, is quite true, "When it comes to a dodge,
the Papists beat us!" Let us take care that we do
not come to a dodge, but hold firmly to the truth.

in the expressions of your zeal; but,"
ye Christian People, "let your modera-
tion [19] be so known unto all men as to
be distinguished by all from coldness
and indifference!" But for this, I should
not have called your attention to such
matters.   At the same time, I would
never choose it to be said that I was
slow, upon an emergency, to lay before
the people committed to my trust, the
CORRUPTIONS OF THE CHURCH OF ROME.

Once more, take advice, take warning,
and recollect ever that Popish doctrines
always fall in with the corrupt devices
and desires of our own hearts [20]. When
we fall into this snare, it is because we
forsake Christ and His commands of

Nathaniel
Marshall's
Serm. iv.
431.

[19] I must not omit to refer here to Puller's " Mode-
ration of the Church of England."   There is a new
and good reprint of it by the Rev. Robert Eden,
1843.

[20] No truer words than Secker's — " It is too well
known that mankind will do any thing rather than
their duty, and part with any thing sooner than their
vices." Vol. vi. p. 370.   His Sermons on Popery, and
Abp. Sharpe's, together with the two small Treatises
of Bp. Bull's, are full of practical information on the
points dwelt upon in this Manual.

holiness. We will not have Him to reign over us! And what then? As it has been strikingly said, "If the God of this world hath not quite blinded us, we shall soon see that we, who boast of our religion all the day long, have also, as Martin Luther used to speak, a Pope in our own belly." Homely is the observation, but much cause had he to know the truth of it who contended, if not always temperately, yet boldly and out of a good conscience, for the Reformation which he tended so much to further.

But, mind ye well, if by a holy Faith and a holy life and repentance unfeigned, we follow on to know the Lord, He has undertaken, and will undertake still, that we shall not greatly fall. And in this sense we have "*an unction from the Holy One,*" knowing all things which chiefly concern our well-being here and hereafter. Wherefore "*Try the spirits whether they be of God.*" "*Prove all things; hold fast to that which is good.*" And what shall I say more? Only this: "*Our Lord Jesus Christ Himself, and*

Farindon's
Serm. ii.
650.

1 John ii.
20.

1 John iv.
1.
1 Thess. v
21.

s

God, even our Father, which hath loved us, and hath given us everlasting consolation and good hope through grace, comfort your hearts, and stablish you in every good word and work."

2 Thess. ii. 16, 17.

SERMON VI.

PART II.

"ARE WE BLIND ALSO?"

" Breviter ergo cæci hujus illuminati commendo mysterium. Ea quippe quæ fecit Dominus noster Jesus Christus stupenda atque miranda, et opera et verba sunt ; opera, quia facta sunt ; verba, quia signa sunt. Si ergo quid significat hoc quod factum est cogitemus, genus humanum est iste cæcus ; hæc enim cæcitas contigit in primo homine per peccatum, de quo omnes originem duximus, non solum mortis sed etiam iniquitatis."—AUGUST. in Joan. Evang., c. ix., Tract xliv., Tom. iii. 589. E.

Ἐγὼ δὲ καὶ εὐηργετῆσθαι αὐτόν φημι ἀπὸ τῆς πηρώσεως, τοὺς γὰρ ἔνδον ἀνέβλεψεν ὀφθαλμούς· τί γὰρ ὄφελός ἐστι τοῖς Ἰουδαίοις τῶν ὀμμάτων; μείζονα γὰρ κόλασιν ἔσχον, πηρωθέντες ἐν τῷ βλέπειν; τί δὲ τούτῳ βλάβος ἀπὸ τῆς πηρώσεως, διὰ γὰρ ταύτης ἀνέβλεψεν· ὥσπερ οὖν τὰ κακὰ οὐκ ἔστι κακὰ τὰ κατὰ τὸν παρόντα βίον, οὕτως οὐδὲ τὰ ἀγαθὰ ἀγαθά· ἀλλ' ἁμαρτία μόνη κακόν, πήρωσις δὲ οὐ κακόν.—CHRYSOST. Hom. lvi. (al. lv.) in loc. tom. iii. 327. C.

Ἡ οὖν ἁμαρτία ὑμῶν μένει. Μένει ἀσύγγνωστος, διότι λέγοντες βλέπειν, οὐ βλέπετε, ἐθελοτυφλώττοντες ὑπὸ φθόνου καὶ πονηρίας. Ἔδειξε τοίνυν ὅτι ἡ σωματικὴ ὅρασις, ἐφ' ᾗ μεγαλαυχοῦσιν, αὐτὴ τούτους καταδικάζει· ἅμα δὲ καὶ τὸν πρὶν τυφλὸν ἐντεῦθεν παρεμυθήσατο, καὶ βεβαιότερον εἰς τὴν πίστιν ἀπειργάσατο.—EUTHYM. ZIGABEN. Comment. in loc.

" Si cœci essetis, id est, si vos cæcos adverteretis, et ad medicum curreretis, si ergo ita cœci essetis, non haberetis peccatum : quia veni ego auferre peccatum. Nunc vero dicitis, quia videmus : peccatum vestrum manet. Quare ? Quia dicendo videmus, medicum non quæritis in cæcitate vestrâ remanetis, hoc est ergo quod paullo ante non intellexeramus, quod ait Ego veni ut qui non vident videant : quid est, ut qui non vident, videant ? Qui se non videre confitentur, et medicum quærunt, ut videant. Et qui vident, cœci fiant : quid est, qui vident, cœci fiant ? Qui se putant videre, et medicum non quærunt in suâ cæcitate permanent."—AUGUSTIN. ut suprà, p. 594. E.

SERMON VI.

PART II.

"ARE WE BLIND ALSO?"

JOHN ix. 40, 41 [1].

" And some of the Pharisees which were with Him
heard these words, and said unto Him, Are we blind
also ?   Jesus said unto them, If ye were blind, ye
should have no sin ; but now ye say, We see ; therefore your sin remaineth."

METHINKS, Christian Brethren, were our
comprehension clear, and our vision un-
warped by the crooked ways of the
world, these words of our blessed Lord
would drive us to search and try our
hearts.   And when I do read in this
beloved Disciple's first Epistle, " *Who-*

---

[1] Preached at West Tarring, Nov. 17, 1850.   The
text is taken from the Second Lesson for the day.

soever is born of God doth not commit sin ; for his seed remaineth in him : and he cannot sin, because he is born of God ;" I am ready to fall upon my knees alway, and to cry out with strong supplication and earnest prayer, *" God be merciful to me a sinner ! "* Moreover, I cannot but haste to apply all those words of St. Paul to myself: *" Behold, thou art called a Jew, and restest in the law, and makest thy boast of God, and knowest His will, and approvest the things that are more excellent, being instructed out of the law ; and art confident that thou thyself art a guide of the blind, a light of them which are in darkness ; an instructor of the foolish, a teacher of babes, which hast the form of knowledge and of the truth in the law. Thou therefore which teachest another, teachest thou not thyself? thou that preachest a man should not steal, dost thou steal? Thou that sayest a man should not commit adultery, dost thou commit adultery? thou that abhorrest idols, dost thou commit sacrilege? thou that makest thy boast of the law,*

1 John iii. 9.

through breaking the law dishonourest thou God? For the name of God is blasphemed among the Gentiles through you, as it is written." Rom. ii 17—24.

Let there be no mistake. What is written in the Scriptures of truth, is written for our warning and instruction in righteousness ;—and what applies to the Jew, in as far forth as it is not ceremonial, but of moral and eternal purpose, applies unto us,—ay, more fully, more directly, more imperatively, if it might be, in proportion to the light vouchsafed to us. And yet, we do profess, and call ourselves Christians [2], and many are they, who in the self-righteousness of their hearts, when they behold the wickedness in the which the world lieth, turn it not to their own mending and

---

[2] "Behold a worse than a Sadducee is here, and that is a Christian Atheist! Oh! give me that word Christian again, that I speak not contradictions." How striking are these words of Lightfoot's!—Works, ii. 1109. Folio. But as Ant. Farindon says, "We do more than the Pope ever did, though he be liberal in his pardons. We grant indulgences to ourselves!" Vol. ii. 1120.

improvement, and as a spur to growth
" *in grace and in the knowledge of our
Lord and Saviour Jesus Christ,*" but
comfort themselves rather that they are
not as other men are ;—standing, as it
were, and praying thus with themselves :
" *God, I thank thee, that I am not as
other men are, extortioners, unjust, adulterers, or even as this publican. I fast
twice in the week, I give tithes of all I
possess ;*"—words which, I need not to
tell you, are compatible with Pharisaic
pride of the heart unrebuked, with unhallowed thoughts, with affection to god-
ward brawny and undisciplined.   And
St. Paul's words, slightly altered, come
home with mighty force—" *He is not a*"
Christian " *which is one outwardly ;
neither is that* " Christianity " *which is
outward in the flesh ; but he is a* " Christian " *which is one inwardly ; and* "
Christianity " *is that of the heart, in the
spirit, and not in the letter ; whose praise
is not of men but of God.*"

God have mercy upon us, " *a sinful
nation laden with iniquity !* "   For, how

Luke xviii.
11, 12.

See Rom.
ii. 28, 29.

Isa. i. 4.

many fearful sins are committed in the light of this sun by such as boast of the name of Christian, and glory (as well they might, if truly and sincerely) in the name of Protestants! Ye Christian People! in the broad day, in the visions of the night, at home and abroad, my heart is troubled for *our* sins, who ought to be, as far as the imperfections of human nature will admit, without sin! For, we are called with a holy calling,— we are baptized into Christ,—the vows of the New Covenant are upon us,—we belong to a Reformed [3], and (in theory) to a Holy Church, "*built upon the foundation of the Apostles and Prophets, Jesus Christ Himself being the chief corner stone.*" But, doth "*all the building fitly framed together*" grow "*unto an holy temple in the Lord? Builded to-*" Eph. 20.

[3] "The whole city, we say, would soon be fair, if every one would but sweep before his own door. And the whole estate would soon be reformed, if each would but do his part, look home to himself, and set seriously upon the amendment of that one whom it concerneth him most to look after."—GATAKER's *Sermons. Dedication to* NOAH's *Faith. Folio*, 1637.

Ephes. ii.
21, 22.

gether for an habitation of God through the Spirit," lead we godly and spiritual lives as though God were in us of a truth? Alas! alas! trouble is never far off for the wickedness [4] of such as dwell in the land, and make their boast of belonging to a pure and Apostolical branch of Christ's Holy Catholic Church! Insomuch so, that they who fear God, and speak often one to another of His praise, might take up the Prophet's sorrowful burden and say, "Oh that my head were waters, and mine eyes a fountain of tears, that I might weep day and night for the slain of the daughter of my people! Oh that I had in the wilderness a lodging of wayfaring men; that I might leave my people, and go from them! for they be all adulterers, an assembly of treacherous

[4] "Papistrie is not only a sin, but a present punishment of God, inflicted on man for sin, specially for contempt of the Gospel: and a procurement of that fearful wrath which is to come, which, if it were considered, men would not esteem Papistrie so indifferent a thing as they do."—BP. COWPER of Galloway's vith Day's Conference of a Catholic with a Roman Catholic.

men. And they bend their tongues like their bow for lies : but they are not valiant for the truth upon the earth ; for they proceed from evil to evil, and they know not Me, saith the Lord." "Shall I not visit them for these things, saith the Lord?" Jer. ix. 1—3. Jer. ix. 9.

Christian Brethren—ye that do protest against the errors heaped on our most Holy Faith,—our *"iniquities have turned away"* our strong confidence, *"and your sins have withholden good things from you. For among My people are found wicked men: they lay wait, as he that setteth snares; they set a trap, they catch men."* It is a sad, sad truth,—many Jer. v. 25 26. that profess and call themselves Christians, and rejoice in the appellation of Protestant, do, as I hinted, make a shift to live pretty much the life of heathens [5];

[5] And hence, when scared and conscience-stricken, they the readier fall back on Rome. What Brevint says in "The Preface" to his "*Saul and Samuel at Endor*," is pithy and true: "Ignorant sinners run generally for shelter to Rome, as broken merchants do to the King's Bench, with hope of being there secured against the ordinary course of justice." I may add, that Brevint's Works contain some remarkable statements, and his residence for seventeen years "amongst

and if a holy life be the fruit, as it is, of a holy Faith—what Faith must theirs be? I cannot but make answer with David, and say, "*The Lord our God made a breach upon us, for that we sought Him not after the due order!*" We have sinned as our fathers have done before us, and for the sins that we have sinned, for those we are punished! "*Breach upon breach*" hath fallen upon us, and in all this let us acknowledge the hand of the Lord for good!

1 Chron. xv. 13.

Job xvi. 14.

And now, methinks, I do hear words muttered in silence, like unto those contained in the text, which have reference, as you know, to that all-beautiful miracle of healing, where the Lord of life gave

the Romanists themselves," gave him great opportunities of forming the conclusions he has sometimes expressed in no measured language. Certainly he did "*fetch out the dirt and ashes which lay hid in the skin of a Sodom when it passed for a golden apple!*" and having been employed to reconcile the two religions, (ineffectually, as is well known,) he had as good cause to know what was "*within the entrails*" of the Romish Church, as those men "*who make it their great business to disguise and paint its outside.*" I am afraid we have too many of these Artists amongst us now!

sight unto the "*man which was blind from his birth*," thereby declaring His Almighty power; for what they said was true—"*Since the world began was it not heard that any man opened the eyes of one that was born blind;*" for although by that skill which God giveth to the leech for the benefit of His creatures, the cataract may be removed from the infant's eye, yet is it beyond man's power to give vision where the nerve and life of vision is not. That is in God's hands only, even as the Psalmist saith, "THE LORD GIVETH SIGHT TO THE BLIND." The "FATHER OF LIGHTS" can alone give light where all was darkness before!

ver. 32.

Ps. cxlv. 7.

But this by the way. And, as I said, methinks I do hear words, like those of the text muttered in silence: "*And some of the Pharisees which were with Him heard these words, and said unto Him, Are we blind also? Jesus said unto them, If ye were blind, ye should have no sin: but now ye say, We see; therefore your sin remaineth.*"

John ix. 40, 41.

Christian Brethren, let us confess our sins [6]. Let us acknowledge our back-slidings, our short-comings, our imperfections, many and manifold. At the present juncture, of which I shall presently speak more fully, let us do so especially. For indeed, to the question, if put, "*Are we blind also?*" I cannot fail to reply—"*Blindness in part has happened*" unto us. We have professed much, and brought in little! We have talked of our good works, and behold evil is before us! As I may apply those

Rom. xi. 25.

---

[6] It is a comforting passage that, in Abp. Abbot's Lectures on the Book of Jonah : " God's Church is made of sinners. Christ Jesus did die for sinners. Our very Creed doth teach us that the ' Communion of Saints ' and the ' Forgiveness of Sins ' must be joined and go together. He who will have part in the one must have his fellowship with the other. He cannot come to the first, but he must taste of the latter. Let the weak then raise up his heart and strengthen his feeble knees. Sinners, which call for grace, do belong to the adoption. Noe swerved, and yet he was a Patriarch. Lot fell, yet he is said by St. Peter to have had a righteous soul. Peter himself had a guilty conscience, and yet he was a great Apostle. Jonas was a mighty trespasser, yet still remained the Lord's Prophet."—Pp. 334, 335, 4to, 1613.

words of Haggai the Prophet, when he reproved the people for neglecting the building of the house. *" Ye looked for much, and lo, it came to little ; and when ye brought it home, I did blow upon it. Why? saith the Lord of Hosts. Because of mine house that is waste, and ye run every man unto his own house."* ^{Hagg.} Simply, we have not been *" jealous "* for the Lord God of Hosts,—for His honour and glory, and the spread of His Holy Word amongst the people ! We have not done all that we might have done to show forth His praise, and therefore others, without a call, and by their intrusive presence, would fain do what we have not done,—being ready to graft upon a people unprepared all sorts of superstitious usages, not only not accompanying salvation, but contrary to *" the simplicity of the Gospel,"* and *" the truth as it is in Jesus ! "*

I do entreat ye, Brethren beloved, listen the more attentively, if I would speak of matters which my long residence amongst you entitles me to speak. None other could speak so plainly as I can and command attention,—none other could speak with more real interest as concerns you all, among whom I have gone out and in these many years, "*witnessing both to small and great*" the truths of that Holy Gospel, in which, and by which, we stand.

Acts xxvi. 22.

Well then! If any ask, "ARE WE BLIND ALSO?" I bid ye look on the unhallowed and profane lives of professing [7] Christians,—I bid ye listen to the Prophet's words : "*Hear, ye deaf; and look, ye blind, that ye may see. Who is blind, but my servant? or deaf, as my messenger that I sent? who is blind as he that is perfect, and blind as the Lord's servant? Seeing many things, but thou observest not; opening the ears, but he heareth not." "Bring forth the blind people that have eyes, and the deaf that*

Isa. xlii. 18—20.

---

[7] It is old Fuller that asks—"What good doth the Ark of God in Shiloh, with Levites attending before it, Aaron's rod, pot of manna, mercy-seat within it, if there be a Sodom in Sion, a Bethaven in Bethel, folly in Israel?"—See Sermon on "*Strange Justice*," p. 21. Ed. 1656.

have ears ! " Now these are striking _{Isa. xliii.} words,—and they may remind us of our ^{8.} own homely proverb, " None so blind as those who will not see." And such blind-ness, muchwise at least, has been ours. We have had our eyes opened to see the great things of our salvation, and oftentimes have shut them close. From the time of the Reformation downwards, we ought to have been a congregation of faithful men, for in our Church " the pure word of God has been preached, and the Sacraments duly ministered ac-cording to Christ's ordinance in all those things that of necessity are requisite to the same." Who then hath " *bewitched* " Art. XIX. us, that so many should not " *obey the truth, before whose eyes Jesus Christ hath been evidently set forth, crucified among you ?* " Christian Brethren, set upon by Gal. iii. 1. Satan, the plague of a man's heart, which is his sin, hath consigned him over to that negligence which is sure to end in the ignorance of God's truth,—and thus it comes about that many " *baptized into Christ* " hold not fast by His Cross, but

T

are taken captive by the world, the flesh, and the devil.

But in the midst of all our sins, God remembereth His everlasting mercies; and even when we say " *we see* " and see not, He bringeth before us such visions as no eye *can* see unmoved. And even thus is it now ; ay, and if we will but hear, in the attack which is made by an intrusive and insolent power on the pure and Apostolical branch of Christ's Holy Catholic Church established in these kingdoms, God yet speaketh in His holiness ! A sound has gone forth, through our sea-girt isle,—the winds and the waves are chartered to bear the sound,—the south repeats it to the north,—county after county rings with it,—the downs and the mountains toss it from height to height,—and it has spread like a beacon or a beltane fire through the length and breadth of the land. " *A voice of noise from the city, a* Isa. lxvi. 6. *voice from the temple*," doth cry, as it were, to Protestant England, and saith, " *Awake, awake* "—arise, thou ancient

nation, and shake thyself, like Samson, Judg. xvi.
in thy strength,—proclaim the name of 20.
the Lord, and His Holy Book, and the
One Mediator between God and man [8]——

[8] I give a striking passage here from Bp. Hacket's
Sermons. It may lead some to his goodly folio.
"Our Gods are not plural ; our Redeemers are not
many. They that have tutelary martyrs for almost
every Church, and patron saints distinctly for every
kingdom, they have so many serpents lifted up, and
they look so many ways that their wounds stink and
are corrupt through their foolishness, and they prosper
no way. We have one Head to which the body is
knit ; one Shepherd to guide the flock ; one Corner-
stone in the building ; one serpent in the wilderness ;
*one Mediator between God and man, the Man Christ
Jesus.* An infinite virtue can admit of no co-partner-
ship. I tremble at their Infidelity that frame Scholas-
tical cases out of their own brain, how others are sub-
servient unto the Son of God in the work of our Redemption. But He says, "*I have trodden the wine-
press alone, and of the people there was none with me.*"—
Isa. lxiii. 3. Whether an *Israelite* chanced to be
stung in the head, or in the face ; whether upon the
breast, or on the lower part of the body, one Serpent
upon the Pole was enough to heal all. So we have
sins original and actual ; of commission and omission ;
of ignorance, infirmity, and presumption ; of thought,
word, and deed : *Undique Morsus ;* we are stung from
the crown of the head to the sole of the foot. But as
all are dead, *so* ONE *died* for all, that they " *which live*

T 2

" stand fast in the liberty with which Christ hath made you free, and be not entangled again in the yoke of " Romish Gal. v. 1. *" bondage."* Say not, ye Christian people, that these things have come upon us without any fault of ours,—yea rather, in this, as in any other plague or visitation, let us see the hand of the Lord revealed,—let us hear His voice from *" the midst,"* so to say, *" of the fire,"* and when we hear, let us obey, and serve Him better for the time to come, if so be the blessed privileges of our Reformed Church may be reserved unto us, and our *" candlestick "* not removed out of its place. In those awful words unto the angel of the Church of Ephesus, *" Remember, therefore, from whence thou art fallen, and repent, and do the first works ; or else I will come unto thee quickly, and will remove thy candlestick out of his* See Rev. ii. 5. *place, except thou repent."*

should not live unto themselves, but unto Him that died for us, and rose again." 2 Cor. v. 15.—*Sermon on John* iii. 14. p. 532.

But yet further to the point. We have for a long time been alarmed by insidious tendencies, which, with the softening down of Papistical errors, have seemed to lead to their admission; neither has our alarm been without reason, and what we feared, has, to our great distress, come suddenly upon us. In violation of the laws of the Catholic Church, and of that portion of it to which Rome herself belongs [9], by an act hitherto without precedent in these realms—at least, subsequent to the Reformation—not only without the demand of our Sovereign Lady the Queen, but in direct opposition to her Coronation oath, which could assent to no such demand,—the Bishop of Rome, commonly called the Pope, by an assumed authority, under a Papal Bull, has been parcelling out the land we live in into districts for Bishops of

[9] This is a portion of an Address I drew up as Rural Dean to present to the Lord Bishop. The point specially alluded to is given in VAN ESPEN, *Jus Eccles. Univ.* i. 162, quoted by the Bishop of London in reply to the President and Fellows of Sion College.

the Romish Church, and has moreover
constituted by (what I called before) an
insolent and intrusive Act, a Cardinal
Archbishop of Westminster, with a delegated authority extending over the
county of Sussex,—all of which only
shows that her Domination in her own
eyes is just what it was, and that on the
point of her Supremacy, and so, of Infallibility [10], she has never budged an
inch, but has been biding her time
quietly in the back ground, though restless as ever on her seven hills.   And
upon her forehead is the name graven
still—" MYSTERY, BABYLON, THE MO-

[10] Laud, in his Conference with Fisher the Jesuit,
speaks to him " of the Pope's boundless ambition, and
this most unchristian brain-sick device, that in all
controversies of the Faith he is infallible, and that by
way of inspiration and prophecy, in the conclusion
which he gives." Sect. 39. v. p. 320.   Ed. Cardwell.

Barrow, let me hint to modern debaters, has hit the
right nail upon the head : " You may call it what you
please, but it is evident that in truth the Papal mo-
narchy is a temporal dominion, driving on worldly
ends by worldly means, such as our Lord never meant
to institute."—On the Pope's Supremacy, Theol. Works,
vii. 263.

THER OF HARLOTS AND ABOMINATIONS ^{Rev. xvii. 5.} OF THE EARTH.

And what then? We, assured of this fact, that "no foreign prince, person, prelate, state, or potentate, hath, or ought to have, any jurisdiction, power, superiority, pre-eminence, or authority, ecclesiastical or spiritual, within this realm,"——we, as Protestants, must not admit of such an aggression on the part of the Vatican, without declaring it to be an invasion of the rights of the Crown, and of the charge of our own Episcopate. From all proper quarters the Queen will be addressed,——from hence, as soon as the Great Council of the Nation shall be assembled, I purpose, with your assistance, to present petitions to both Houses of Parliament [11], expressive of our freest indignation, and with a resolution, most dogged and most determined, to resist that intrusive power which has not only insulted our Sovereign Lady the Queen, but which would

[11] The petitions were duly presented, and in proper course.

take the Bible out of the hands of our
people, causing them to err "concerning
Purgatory, Pardons, Worshipping, and
Adoration, as well of Images as of Re-
Art.XXII. liques, and also Invocation of Saints,"—
to say nothing of the Worship of the
Virgin, and that Massing, which is so
near to idolatry as in my judgment to
be all but inseparable from it.

With such words of soberness, and,
as I believe, of truth, have I thought it
right to address you on the present occasion,—going out of my usual track,
which is to dwell upon matters accompanying salvation,—Christ crucified, a holy
Faith and a holy life, and charity which
is the end of the commandment. I add
yet a word more of deep import. If we
say " *We see*,"—we have been delivered
from the night of Papal darkness,—let
us be sure we do. If we say we are a
Reformed Church,—let us live reformed
lives; for, depend upon it, than an unholy
and an ungodly life there is no greater
heresy! If we lift up our voices and
cry "NO POPERY," let us lift up our

hearts withal unto the Lord, and beseech Him, Who alone can, to "absolve" His "people from their offences, that through" His "bountiful goodness we may all be delivered from the bands of those sins, which by our frailty we have committed." To cry "NO POPERY" _{24th Sund. after Trin.} with an unhallowed and an uncharitable voice, is but to offer a sacrifice without a heart, and to go on in our own sin whilst we are reproving others, is to avail no more than those ignorant ones did "*who all with one voice about the space of two hours cried out, Great is Diana of the Ephesians.*" _{Acts xix. 34.}

Thou Christian man! that sayest "*I see,*" remember what was said to the Church of the Laodiceans,—that luke-warm Church, nor cold, nor hot,— "*Anoint thine eyes with eyesalve that thou mayest see* [12]?" _{Rev. iii. 18.}

[12] Good reader! Christian reader! I have pondered on these words of Laud: "It is time to end, especially for me, that have so many things of weight lying upon me, and disabling me from these polemic discourses, beside the burden of sixty-five" (in my case, forty-five) "years complete, which draws on

apace to the period set by the prophet David (Ps. xc. 10), and to the time that I must go and give God and Christ an account of the talent committed to my charge : in which God, for Christ Jesus' sake, be merciful to me ; who knows that, however in many weaknesses, yet I have with a faithful and single heart (bound to His free grace for it) laboured the meeting, the blessed meeting, of truth and peace in His Church ; and which God, in His own good time, will (I hope) effect. To Him be all honour and praise for ever. Amen." — *Conclusion of Conference with Fisher the Jesuit.*

THE END.

GILBERT & RIVINGTON, Printers, St. John's Square, London.

By the same Author,

Just published, Second Edition,

PASTORAL LETTER on the NEW ROMAN CATHOLIC AGGRESSION after the OLD FASHION.

———

I. EARLY PIETY. In 18mo. Price 2s. A PLAIN CHRISTIAN'S MANUAL ; or, SIX SERMONS on Early Piety, the Sacraments, and Man's Latter End ; Uncontroversial, but suited to the present Time.

Also, an EDITION on Fine Paper, with NOTES. Price 3s. 6d. in cloth boards.

II. "NO PROPHECY of the SCRIPTURE is of any PRIVATE INTERPRETATION." A Sermon delivered at the Ordinary Visitation of the Archdeaconry of Chichester, in the Deanery of Storrington, July 19, 1849. In 8vo. price 1s. 6d.

III. PLAIN PRACTICAL SERMONS. 2 vols. 8vo. price 26s.

IV. The TEACHING of the PRAYER BOOK. Price 7s. 6d.

V. ASSIZE SERMONS, preached at the Lent and Summer Assizes, Lewes, 1845. Price 2s. 6d.

VI. A SERMON, preached at the Re-opening of Patching Church, July 12, 1835.

VII. "THE SUN SHALL BE TURNED INTO DARKNESS. A Sermon preached on the occasion of the Eclipse, May 15, 1836.

VIII. "HOLY MATRIMONY." A Sermon, with Notes and Appendix. 1837.

IX. The UNCONTROVERSIAL PREACHING of the PAROCHIAL CLERGY, enforced from the Beatitudes. Price 1s. 6d.

X. "AND THE SEA GAVE UP THE DEAD THAT WERE IN IT." A SERMON, preached at West Tarring, December 1, 1850, being the Sunday after the awful Calamity in the Worthing Roads. Profits, if any, for the Poor Families. Price 2d.

———

RIVINGTONS,

ST. PAUL'S CHURCH YARD, AND WATERLOO PLACE.

Also, Edited by the same Author,

Vols. VI. and VII. of the DOCTOR, &c. By the late ROBERT SOUTHEY. Post 8vo. Vol. VI., price 10*s.* 6*d.*; Vol. VII., 14*s.*

The DOCTOR, &c. In one vol., price 21*s.*

SOUTHEY'S COMMON PLACE BOOK. FIRST SERIES.—CHOICE PASSAGES. Price 18*s.*

SOUTHEY'S COMMON PLACE BOOK. SECOND SERIES.—SPECIAL COLLECTIONS. Price 18*s.*

SOUTHEY'S COMMON PLACE BOOK. THIRD SERIES.—ANALYTICAL READINGS. Price 21*s.*

SOUTHEY'S COMMON PLACE BOOK. FOURTH SERIES.—ORIGINAL MEMORANDA. Price 21*s.*

LONDON:

LONGMAN, BROWN, GREEN, AND LONGMANS.

APRIL, 1851.

NEW BOOKS

RECENTLY PUBLISHED

BY

Messrs. RIVINGTON,

ST. PAUL'S CHURCH YARD, AND WATERLOO PLACE.

I.

THE Second Series of OCCASIONAL SERMONS on CHURCH QUESTIONS of the DAY, preached in Westminster Abbey. By CHRISTOPHER WORDSWORTH, D.D., Canon of Westminster. CONTENTS :—1. Diotrephes and St. John : on the claim of the Bishop of Rome to exercise Jurisdiction in England and Wales, by erecting therein Episcopal Sees.—2. St. Peter at Antioch, and the Roman Pontiff in England.—3. The Christian Soldier a Christian Builder.—4. The Recent Proposal of the Church of Rome to make a New Article of Faith.—5. Church Synods.—6. Secessions to the Church of Rome.—7. The Privileges and Duties of the Laity. In 8vo. 8s.

Lately published, The FIRST SERIES. *New Edition*, 8s.

II.

SICKNESS; its TRIALS and BLESSINGS. *Second Edition*. In small 8vo. 6s. An APPENDIX is now added, (which may be had separately) containing Suggestions to Persons in Attendance on the Sick and Dying.

III.

JOURNAL of a TOUR in ITALY in 1850, with an Account of an INTERVIEW with the POPE, at the Vatican. By the Rev. GEORGE TOWNSEND, D.D., Canon of Durham. In post 8vo. *Second Edition*, 7s. 6d.

IV.

The ENGLISH ORDINAL; its History, Validity, and Catholicity. With an Introduction on the Three Holy Orders of Ministers in the Church. By the Rev. MACKENZIE F. C. WALCOTT, M.A., Curate of St. James's, Westminster. In post 8vo. 10s. 6d.

V.

A New Volume of TWENTY-FOUR SHORT LECTURES on the CHURCH CATECHISM. By the Ven. EDWARD BERENS, M.A., Archdeacon of Berks. In 12mo. 4s. 6d.

VI.

The THEOLOGICAL CRITIC; a Quarterly Journal. Edited by the Rev. T. K. ARNOLD, M.A., Rector of Lyndon, and late Fellow of Trinity College, Cambridge. This Journal will embrace Theology in its widest acceptation, and several articles of each number will be devoted to Biblical Criticism. CONTENTS of No. I.:—1. Newman's Ninth Lecture.—2. Galatians iii. 13.— 3. Cardinal Bessarion.—4. Lepsius on Biblical Chronology.— 5. The Ministry of the Body.—6. Romans xiv.—7. Is the Beast from the Sea the Papacy?—8. Modern Infidelity: Miss Martineau and Mr. Atkinson.—9. St. Columban and the Early Irish Missionaries.—10. Dr. Bloomfield and Mr. Alford.—11. " Things Old and New." In 8vo. 4s.

VII.

The ELEMENTS of NATURAL THEOLOGY. By JAMES BEAVEN, D.D., Professor of King's College, Toronto. In small 8vo. 5s.

VIII.

The ORATION of DEMOSTHENES on the CROWN. Edited from the best Text, with ENGLISH NOTES, and Grammatical References. By the Rev. THOMAS KERCHEVER ARNOLD, M.A., Rector of Lyndon, and late Fellow of Trinity College, Cambridge. In 12mo. 4s. 6d.

Also, by the same Editor, with English Notes, uniformly printed, The OLYNTHIAC ORATIONS of DEMOSTHENES. 3s.

IX.

The CHRISTIAN CHARACTER; Six Sermons preached in Lent. By JOHN JACKSON, M.A., Rector of St. James's, Westminster. *Third Edition.* 4s.

X.

The FAIR ISLAND: a Descriptive Poem on the Isle of WIGHT. By EDMUND PEEL, Esq., Author of " The Return," " Judge Not," &c. 5s.

XI.

HOMERI ILIAS, Lib. I—IV., with a CRITICAL INTRODUCTION, and copious ENGLISH NOTES. By the Rev. THOMAS KERCHEVER ARNOLD, M.A., Rector of Lyndon, and late Fellow of Trinity College, Cambridge. In 12mo. 7s. 6d.

XII.

A NEW HARMONY of the GOSPELS, in the Form of LECTURES. By the Rev. L. VERNON HARCOURT, M.A. In 3 vols. 8vo. 2l. 8s.

XIII.

The HANDBOOK of FRENCH VOCABULARY. 4s. 6d.
The HANDBOOK of GERMAN VOCABULARY. 4s.

These Vocabularies contain a Collection of Nouns and Verbs, with their usual combinations, and a carefully arranged Selection of the most necessary Words and Phrases. They are edited (from the German of Dr. CARL PLÖTZ) by the Rev. THOMAS KERCHEVER ARNOLD, M.A., Rector of Lyndon, and late Fellow of Trinity College, Cambridge.

XIV.

The WEDDING GIFT; a DEVOTIONAL MANUAL for the MARRIED, or those intending to Marry. By WILLIAM EDWARD HEYGATE, M.A. In 18mo. 3s.

XV.

A NEW HARMONY of the FOUR EVANGELISTS, in Parallel Columns, in the words of the Authorized Version. By the Rev. ISAAC WILLIAMS, B.D., late Fellow of Trinity College, Oxford. In small 8vo. 8s. 6d.

₊ This Work forms a Companion and Key to the Commentary and Harmony of the Gospels, by the same Author, in Seven Volumes, just completed.

XVI.

A HISTORY of the ARTICLES of RELIGION : to which is added a SERIES of DOCUMENTS, from A. D. 1536 to A. D. 1615; together with Illustrations from Contemporary Sources. By CHARLES HARDWICK, M.A., Fellow of St. Catharine's Hall, Cambridge, and Whitehall Preacher. In 8vo. 10s. 6d.

XVII.

CATECHESIS ; or, CHRISTIAN INSTRUCTION preparatory to CONFIRMATION and FIRST COMMUNION. Forming an Introduction to, and printed uniformly with, Dr. Wordsworth's *Theophilus Anglicanus.* By the Rev. CHARLES WORDSWORTH, M.A., Warden of Trinity College, Glenalmond. *Second Edition.* Post 8vo. 5s. 6d.

XVIII.

The CHURCH in the WORLD ; or, the LIVING AMONG the DEAD. By the Rev. J. BAINBRIDGE SMITH, M.A., late of St. John's College, Cambridge, Professor and Vice President of King's College, Windsor, Nova Scotia. In small 8vo. 3s.

XIX.

The **FIRST GREEK BOOK**; on the plan of "Henry's First Latin Book." By the Rev. THOMAS KERCHEVER ARNOLD, M.A., Rector of Lyndon, and late Fellow of Trinity College, Cambridge. *Second Edition.* 5s.

XX.

The **THEORY of BAPTISM**; or, the **REGENERATION** of INFANTS in BAPTISM vindicated on the Testimony of HOLY SCRIPTURE, CHRISTIAN ANTIQUITY, and the CHURCH of ENGLAND. By the Rev. GEORGE CROLY, LL.D., Rector of the United Parishes of St. Stephen's, Walbrook, and St. Benet, London. In 8vo. 8s.

XXI.

The **CHURCH APOSTOLIC, PRIMITIVE, and ANGLICAN**: a Series of SERMONS. By the Rev. JOHN COLLINGWOOD, M.A., Minister of Duke-street Episcopal Chapel, Westminster; one of the Masters of Christ's Hospital, and Editor of Bishop Hobart's Companion to the Altar. In 8vo. 9s.

XXII.

LONGER LATIN EXERCISES, PART II.; containing a Selection of Passages of greater length, in genuine idiomatic English, for Translation into Latin. By the Rev. THOMAS KERCHEVER ARNOLD, M.A., Rector of Lyndon, and late Fellow of Trinity College, Cambridge. In 8vo. 4s.
Lately published, THE FIRST PART. 4s.

XXIII.

The **SECOND PART of a PRACTICAL INTRODUCTION to GREEK PROSE COMPOSITION.** (On the PARTICLES.) In this Part the Passages for Translation are of considerable length. By the Rev. THOMAS KERCHEVER ARNOLD, M.A., Rector of Lyndon, and late Fellow of Trinity College, Cambridge. In 8vo. 6s. 6d.

Also, by the same Author,

The SEVENTH EDITION of the FIRST PART. In 8vo. 6s. 6d.

XXIV.

ERUVIN; or, MISCELLANEOUS ESSAYS on Subjects connected with the NATURE, HISTORY, and DESTINY of MAN. By the Rev. S. R. MAITLAND, D.D., F.R.S. and F.S.A. *Second Edition.* In small 8vo. 5s. 6d.

XXV.

FAMILY READING; or, the NEW TESTAMENT NAR-
RATIVE harmonized and explained by the Bishops and Doctors
of the Church of England. Compiled from various Authors, by
the Hon. Sir EDWARD CUST. In 8vo. 1*l*. 1*s*.

Lately published, by the same Author (uniformly printed),
The FIRST SERIES; on the PROPER LESSONS from the
OLD TESTAMENT, for the Sundays throughout the Year.
8vo. 15*s*.

XXVI.

THEOPHILUS ANGLICANUS; or, Instruction concern-
ing the Church and the Anglican Branch of it. For the use of
Schools, Colleges, and Candidates for Holy Orders. By CHR.
WORDSWORTH, D.D., Canon of Westminster. *Sixth Edition*.
In post 8vo. 8*s*. 6*d*.

XXVII.

SERMONS on the HOLY DAYS of the CHURCH. By
the Rev. J. H. PINDER, M.A., Precentor of Wells Cathedral,
and Principal of Wells Theological College. In 12mo. 7*s*. 6*d*.

Lately published, by the same Author,
SERMONS on the BOOK OF COMMON PRAYER. *Third
Edition*. 7*s*.

XXVIII.

INSTRUCTIONS for the USE of CANDIDATES for
HOLY ORDERS, and of the PAROCHIAL CLERGY, as to
Ordination, Licences, Induction, Pluralities, Residence, &c. &c.;
with Acts of Parliament relating to the above, and Forms to be
used. By CHRISTOPHER HODGSON, M.A., Secretary to
His Grace the Archbishop of Canterbury. *Seventh Edition*. In
8vo. 12*s*.

The additions and improvements in this Edition include a more
convenient arrangement of the Powers enabling Incumbents to
mortgage their Benefices, and to purchase, sell, and exchange
Houses and Lands, and for providing Residences; the recent
Plurality Act, with a Summary; and other information of importance to the Clergy and their Solicitors or Agents.

XXIX.

The PRIVILEGES, DUTIES, and DANGERS in the
ENGLISH BRANCH of the CHURCH of CHRIST at the
Present Time: Six Sermons, preached at Canterbury Cathedral,
in September and October, 1850. By BENJAMIN HARRISON,
M.A., Archdeacon of Maidstone, and Canon of Canterbury. In
8vo. 5*s*. 6*d*.

XXX.

PATRIARCHAL TIMES ; or, the LAND of CANAAN :
in Seven Books. Comprising interesting Events, Incidents, and
Characters, founded on the Holy Scriptures. By Miss
O'KEEFFE. In small 8vo. *Seventh Edition.* 6s. 6d. (*Just
Published.*)

XXXI.

TWENTY-ONE PRAYERS, composed from the Psalms,
for the SICK and AFFLICTED. With other Forms of Prayer.
and a few Hints on the Visitation of the Sick. By the Rev.
JAMES SLADE, M.A., Vicar of Bolton. *Sixth Edition.* 3s. 6d.

XXXII.

The BOY'S ARITHMETIC. PART I. By the Rev.
CHARLES ARNOLD, M.A., Rector of Tinwell, and late Fellow
of Caius College, Cambridge.

The object of this book is to make Arithmetic easier to little
boys, by enabling them to understand it, and to prevent their
forgetting a rule as soon as they have entered upon a new one.
Second Edition. In 12mo. 3s. 6d.

Recently published, The SECOND PART. 3s. 6d.

XXXIII.

A NEW EDITION of The BOOK of COMMON PRAYER
and ADMINISTRATION of the SACRAMENTS, with copious
NOTES, Practical and Historical, from approved Writers of the
Church of England; including the Canons and Constitutions of
the Church. Selected and arranged by RICHARD MANT, D.D.,
late Lord Bishop of Down, Connor, and Dromore.

** This Work is printed verbatim from the Quarto Edition,
and uniformly with D'Oyly and Mant's Family Bible, and forms
a suitable companion to it. In one Volume, super-royal 8vo.
Price 1l. 5s.

** *The* QUARTO *Edition may still be had, price* 1l. 16s.

XXXIV.

The REMAINS of the late Rev. HENRY FRANCIS
LYTE, Incumbent of Lower Brixham, Devon ; with a PREFA-
TORY MEMOIR by the EDITOR. In small 8vo. 8s.

XXXV.

The ATHENIAN STAGE : a Handbook for the Student.
From the German of Witzschel, by the Rev. R. B. PAUL, M.A.,
and the Rev. T. K. ARNOLD, M.A. In 12mo. (*With a Plan of
a Greek Theatre.*) 4s.

XXXVI.

A GENERAL VIEW of the DOCTRINE of REGENE-RATION in BAPTISM. By CHRISTOPHER BETHELL, D.D., Lord Bishop of Bangor. *Fifth Edition.* In 8vo. 9s.

XXXVII.

A SAFE PATH for HUMBLE CHURCHMEN; in SIX SERMONS on the CHURCH CATECHISM, adapted to the Complexion of the Times. By JOHN MILLER, M.A., of Worcester College, Oxford. In 8vo. 4s. 6d.

XXXVIII.

HANDBOOK of MODERN GEOGRAPHY and HIS-TORY. Translated from the German of Pütz, by the Rev. R. B. PAUL, M.A., late Fellow of Exeter College, Oxford; and edited by the Rev. T. K. ARNOLD, M.A., Rector of Lyndon, and late Fellow of Trinity College, Cambridge. In 12mo. 5s. 6d.

*** This Volume completes the Series of Professor Pütz's Handbooks.

Lately published, by the same Editors, (uniformly printed,)
The HANDBOOK of ANCIENT GEOGRAPHY and HIS-TORY. 6s. 6d.
The HANDBOOK of MEDIÆVAL GEOGRAPHY and HISTORY. 4s. 6d.

XXXIX.

ENGLISH BALLADS, and other Poems. By Lord JOHN MANNERS. In small 8vo. 4s.

XL.

The CHRISTIAN LIFE: a Manual of Sacred Verse. By the Rev. ROBERT MONTGOMERY, M.A., Author of "The Omnipresence of the Deity." *Third Edition.* In a pocket volume. 5s.

XLI.

FAMILY READING; or, the NEW TESTAMENT NARRATIVE arranged and explained from the Writings of the Bishops and Doctors of the Church of England. By the Hon. Sir EDWARD CUST. In 8vo. 1l. 1s.

Lately published, by the same Author (uniformly printed),
SUNDAY NIGHT READING, made applicable to the PROPER LESSONS from the OLD TESTAMENT, for the Sundays throughout the Year. 8vo. 15s.

XLII.

HOLY THOUGHTS: a **TREASURY** of **TRUE RICHES**, collected chiefly from our Old Writers. *Fifth Edition.* In pocket size. 1s. 6d.

XLIII.

PRIVATE PRAYERS. Compiled by **WALTER FARQUHAR HOOK,** D.D., Vicar of Leeds. *Fifth Edition.* In 18mo. 2s.

Lately published, by the same Author,
The BOOK of FAMILY PRAYER. *Fifth Edition.* 2s.

XLIV.

A **HANDBOOK** of **GREEK SYNONYMES.** From the French of A. PILLON, Librarian of the Bibliothèque Royale, Paris. Edited, with Notes, by the Rev. T. K. ARNOLD, M.A., Rector of Lyndon, and late Fellow of Trinity College, Cambridge. In 12mo. 6s. 6d.

XLV.

HYMNS and **POEMS** for the **SICK** and **SUFFERING.** In connexion with the Service for the VISITATION of the SICK. Edited by the Rev. T. V. FOSBERY, M.A., Perpetual Curate of Sunningdale. *Second Edition.* In small 8vo. 7s. 6d.

This Volume contains 233 separate pieces : of which about 90 are by writers who lived prior to the 18th Century : the rest are modern, and some of these original. Amongst the names of the writers (between 70 and 80 in number) occur those of Sir J. Beaumont—Sir T. Browne—F. Davison—Elizabeth of Bohemia—P. Fletcher—G. Herbert—Dean Hickes—Bp. Ken—Norris—Quarles—Sandys—Bp. J. Taylor—Henry Vaughan—and Sir H. Wotton. And of modern writers :—Miss E. B. Barrett—The Bishop of Oxford—S. T. Coleridge—Sir R. Grant—Miss E. Taylor—W. Wordsworth—Rev. Messrs. Chandler—Keble—Lyte—Monsell—Moultrie—and Trench.

XLVI.

ESSAYS on **SUBJECTS** connected with the **REFORMATION** in ENGLAND. (*Reprinted from the* BRITISH MAGAZINE, *with Additions.*) By the Rev. S. R. MAITLAND, D.D., F.R.S., Author of " Essays on the Dark Ages." In 8vo. 15s.

XLVII.

COMFORT for the **AFFLICTED.** Selected from various Authors. Edited by the Rev. C. E. KENNAWAY. With a Preface by S. WILBERFORCE, D.D., Lord Bishop of Oxford. *Fifth Edition.* 5s.

Check Out More Titles From HardPress Classics Series In this collection we are offering thousands of classic and hard to find books. This series spans a vast array of subjects – so you are bound to find something of interest to enjoy reading and learning about.

Subjects:
Architecture
Art
Biography & Autobiography
Body, Mind &Spirit
Children & Young Adult
Dramas
Education
Fiction
History
Language Arts & Disciplines
Law
Literary Collections
Music
Poetry
Psychology
Science
…and many more.

Visit us at www.hardpress.net